BOOKKEEPING ACCOUNTING Explained for Small Business & Home Business the Easy Way (Over 25+ Examples!)

Calvin K. Lee, MBA, CPA, CA, CPA (Illinois)

©2016

All Rights Reserved

This book is dedicated to all the accounting partners and colleagues I've had the privilege to work with.

Bookkeeping & Accounting Explained for Small Business & Home Business the Easy Way (Over 25+ Examples)
First Edition, July 2016

Author: Calvin K. Lee

This book or any portion thereof may not be reproduced or used without written permission of the author/publisher except in brief quotations, book reviews, and articles.

Copyright ©2016 Calvin K. Lee
All rights reserved

ISBN 13: 978-1535188272

Praise for Calvin's books

"Thank you so much for the book. This is amazing. You are a very productive author and I have lots to learn from you." - H.W., Ph.D

"I'm 100% certain to say that this book should be accounting 100 pre-requisite course for anyone who wants to take introduction to accounting! Very clear, concise, and concrete. Well done!"

- K.T., CPA, CA

"Calvin has done a great job simplifying these rather complex concepts. Well worth reading if you manage your own business." - Joe Fayt, Professor at Schulich School of Business, York University

"Very comprehensive and easy to read." - Karim A., CPA, CA

"I highly recommend Calvin's book. It is very practical and useful. You can download it during its free book promotion, but you can wait until it's not free and download a paid copy to truly experience its value." - S.A., MBA

*"I accidentally purchased this book not knowing there was a basics book that came first. Even though that is the case, I was expecting textbook-like explanations to accounting that I distinctly remember from my classes. It's a nice feeling when someone realizes they need to

explain the basics to you, yet they are willing to backtrack to wherever the starting point may be. I still struggle with the CPA terminology and basics, but I would rather read small, casual books than learn from a class or official textbook. Learning accounting outside of school has been much more interesting." - Eric

"I like how this book gave you the basics of accounting in a easy to understand manner. It went a little further in detail all the while keeping to the point. This book made accounting basics easy to understand for me. A must read for those who are hesitant to jump in to financials and also want to learn more about accounting in their own business. The book includes a lot of examples and bonus chapters. I'm glad I bought it and consider this book an asset. Totally recommend it." - Life Adventurer

"I want to learn from your great works!" - L.W., MBA

"Great book. Short and simple, straight to the point." - T.H.

"This is awesome! I love the short chapters with clear examples."

"Thank you so much for your hard work. I look forward to using it!" - S.W., MBA

"Very practical, good reading!"

"I really enjoy your books."

"Well done, very informative. I like how you used your example."

"By using his own example, Calvin gives hope for the readers."

"Great real life experience that you can relate to easily."

"Very clear, concise, and concrete. Well done."

"Practical tips and relatable examples. A pleasant read. Congratulations on your recent publications! Keep writing more."

"I've taken notes on my smart phone and will implement them in my life."

"Thanks for the little pearls of wisdom and optimism."

FREE CONTENT

See my website, blog and podcasts for free content on my website.
Topics include accounting, inspirational, wealth, health, love & relationships, career success, and technology.

>>>www.hellocalvinlee.com<<<

To thank you for reading this book, go to my website to download a FREE eBooks on Stress Management and "How to Work Smarter, Not Harder" using this link:

>>>www.hellocalvinlee.com/eBook<<<

Table of Contents

Praise for Calvin's books 4

Preface 12

Introduction 14

Bank Reconciliation 16

Month-end or Year-end Accruals 19

Mortgage or Loan amortization: Method 1 21

Mortgage or Loan amortization: Method 2 24

Recording Amortization (Depreciation) of Tangible Capital Assets 26

Recording Term Deposits, and Interest Received from Term Deposits or GIC's 29

Recording Investments, Dividends & Interest Received from Investments 31

Recording a Return of Capital from an Investment 33

Adjusting an Investment to Fair Market Value 34

Recording Dividend Payments to Shareholders 36

Closing Dividends into Retained Earnings 37

How to Determine Bad Debts Amounts (Uncollectible Accounts Receivable): Method 1 38

How to Determine Bad Debts Amounts (Uncollectible Accounts Receivable): Method 2 40

Writing-off Bad Debts 41

Setting up Allowance for Doubtful Accounts 43

Setting up Accounting Software 45

Getting Started with Accounting Software 46

Trial Balance 48

Creating a New Company 49

Report and Form Options... 50

Account Class.. 52

Customers & Vendors Setup 53

Final thoughts.. 54

About the Author 56

Note to the reader... 57

Contact the author 58

Books by Calvin K. Lee 59

BONUS book #1: 61

"How to Increase Confidence and Succeed in Meeting People: Business Networking the Easy Way…Meet New People Now!" 61

BONUS book #2: 79

"Living an Extraordinary and Amazingly Purposeful Life: 9 Principles to a Better Life" 79

BONUS book #3: 103

"Words of Wisdom, Encouragement, and Inspiration" 103

BONUS book #4: 133

"How to Work Smarter, Not Harder: Success in the Workplace" 133

BONUS book #5: 163

"A Collection of Short Stories" 163

FREE book sample from: 184

"Bookkeeping and Accounting Step-by-step Basics for Small & Medium sized Businesses and Home Businesses: Over 20 Examples of Common Accounting Transactions!" 184

FREE book sample from: 192

"Understanding Financial Statement Analysis for Accountants, Business Owners, Investors, and Stakeholders" 192

BONUS BOOK #6: 204

"LEAP before you THINK" 204

FREE Book sample from 220

"TIME MANAGEMENT: saving 4 HOURS a week" 220

FREE book sample from: 228

From Ordinary to Extraordinary: 228

How God Used Ordinary Men and Women in the Bible 228

About the Author 246

Contact the author 248

Other books by Calvin K. Lee 249

THANK YOU! 250

Bookkeeping & Accounting Explained

Preface
By Joe Fayt

There are so many great books published each year, many of them by Canadians. But few authors have published great books in such a wide variety of disciplines. Calvin Lee is one of those rare authors. He has published books on so many interesting topics including time management, finding purpose in life, building self-confidence, finance and accounting, and also several works of fiction.

I got to know Calvin in my role as a Marketing Instructor and Case Competition Coach at the Schulich School of Business. He was completing his MBA and I had the opportunity to work with him as he engaged in various competitions, both as a competitor and also as a judge. He was invited to support several undergrad teams as they prepared for the JDC, a very intense case competition sponsored by the Canadian Association of Business Students, with the accounting team winning first place.

Calvin graduated from the Schulich MBA program on the Dean's Honor List, and received a graduation award and scholarship from the Dean for outstanding academic achievement and extracurricular involvement. Since graduation he has continued to express his passion for writing and publishing. This latest book is a must-read for anyone who is running a small or home business who needs to understand the key principles of accounting. He has taken a very complex subject and simplified it, making it accessible to anyone. He uses very simple and practical examples to explain all of the basic accounting principles, and more importantly, how to apply them to your business.

If you are currently running your own business, or plan to do so in the near future, I would encourage you to buy this book and read it carefully. It will give you the basics, and serve as a practical reference to go back to when you need help with a specific topic. With his clear and concise style, Calvin will ensure that you can learn everything you need to know about accounting in as little time as possible, so you can spend most of your time doing what you love to do.

Joe Fayt

Marketing Instructor and MBA Case Competition Coach, Schulich School of Business (York University)

Owner, Think Like a Marketer Training Systems

Introduction

Bookkeeping & Accounting are professions that are growing rapidly in popularity. From the time I graduated from my accounting program many years ago to today, the sizes of accounting class graduates have increased many fold. Accounting is considered a stable profession, one that is less prone to layoffs compared to some other industries and professions. This is because no matter how bad the economy gets, every company needs an accountant to maintain its books and records.

Many of my clients are entrepreneurs or small business owners. Many of them do not understand basic bookkeeping and accounting principles and techniques. Accounting is daunting to a lot of people, and it takes years of university studies and professional certification programs to become a CPA. Most people just want basic bookkeeping skills to maintain the accounting records for their company.

If that description fits you, this is the right book for you. You may be a part-time bookkeeper or an accountant in a company that needs to refresh your accounting skills. Textbooks are thick and difficult to understand. You want a quick reference guide for the most common accounting situations. If you've read my book "Bookkeeping & Accounting Basics for Small Business & Home Business", which as an overview of bookkeeping & accounting, this book is a continuation with more examples on specific accounting transactions not covered in that book.

If you want to learn more about understanding Financial Statement Analysis, this book may interest you:

<u>Understanding Financial Statement Analysis: For Accountants, Business Owners, Investors, and Stakeholders</u>.

That's what this book is, it is a short, easy-to read bookkeeping and accounting quick reference guide filled with examples of every-day journal entries bookkeepers do. The over 25+ examples are designed to help you understand accounting concepts effortlessly so you can get back to your busy day.

In this book you will learn effortlessly how to do bank reconciliations, record loan/mortgage amortization, record amortization/depreciation of capital assets, record investments and related investment income, recording bad debts, setting up allowance for doubtful accounts, and much more. As a bonus, I have included sections on how to set up accounting software from scratch.

As a Canadian CPA, Chartered Accountant (CA), and U.S. Certified Public Accountant, I have worked in a Big 4 accounting firm, as well as medium and small-sized accounting firms for a decade.

Clients come to me from all kinds of industries, for example professional associations (i.e. pharmacy association), hospitals, the construction industry, consulting professionals, entertainment industry, senior care homes, non-profit organizations, and professional corporations (doctors, lawyers, dentists, engineers), just to name a few. I have done bookkeeping, accounting, and auditing for numerous clients.

You are busy. So let's turn the page and get started.

Bank Reconciliation

The bank reconciliation is the most basic bookkeeping task. When I first started my career in an accounting firm a decade ago, my first task was to do bank reconciliations for a client. One per month meant I did twelve bank reconciliations.

Bank reconciliations are easy to do. The concept is simple and straight forward.

When a bookkeeper does bookkeeping, he or she records the deposits and records the cheques written. So why does a bookkeeper or accountant need to do a bank reconciliation? It's because of timing difference at month end, quarter-end, or year-end between the bookkeeping records (also called a General Ledger), and the bank statement.

Example.

Let's say in the month of December two cheques were written. One cheque was written on December 10, and another cheque written on December 26. The cheque that was written December 10 was deposited in the same month, so no timing difference between the General Ledger and the bank statement. However, the cheque written on December 26 wasn't deposited until January 4 the next year.

Now we have a timing difference.

Let's say on Dec 1, the bank and General Ledger balance was $100. The cheque written on December 10 was $20, so both the General Ledger and bank statement decreased by $20 to a balance of $80. If the cheque written December 26 was for $30, the General Ledger would decrease to $50. However, the bank statement ending December 31 would still say $80 in the bank because the cheque has not cleared.

To do the bank reconciliation at December 31, you would do this:

Balance per bank: $ 80

Outstanding cheques: (30)

Balance per GL: $ 50

And that's how you do a bank reconciliation.

The same thing is done for outstanding deposits that have been recorded in the bank statement, but not in the General Ledger.

Example.

If a deposit should belong to the month of December, but it didn't enter the bank until January 2, the following would be the bank reconciliation:

Balance before o/s deposit: $ 50

Outstanding deposit: 30

Balance per General Ledger: $ 80

Remember: The goal of the bank reconciliation is to record an expense or deposit in the correct month it pertains to, regardless of when it actually clears the bank. If a cheque is written in December, the bank balance needs to be adjusted to reflect the December cheque even if it doesn't clear the bank until after the

month. Similar for a deposit. If it pertains to a certain month but doesn't get deposited until the first few days of the next month, the balance needs to be adjusted to reflect that.

Month-end or Year-end Accruals

Principle: Sometimes a payment for a month is not paid until the next month. For example, payroll taxes to be remitted to the government. The payroll taxes for April won't be remitted to the government until May. However, the amount of payroll taxes need to be accrued in the month of April otherwise the expenses would be understated.

Example.

If the payroll taxes payable for April is $3,000, an accrual needs to be set up on April 30:

Dr. Payroll taxes expense   3,000

   Cr. Payroll taxes payable   3,000

To accrue payroll taxes for the month of April.

What if the payroll saddles the month-end? What if a payroll period of 10 days only 8 days pertain to April, and 2 days pertain to May?

Example.

In that case, the payroll taxes as well as the payroll payable must be pro-rated for the month of April and recorded as such in April. If the payroll taxes for the entire 10 days is $3,000, 8 days would mean $2,400 pertain to April (8/10 x $3,000 = $2,400) and the remaining $600 pertain to May.

Therefore, the journal entry would be:

Dr. Payroll taxes expense 2,400

Cr. Payroll taxes payable 2,400

To accrue payroll taxes for the month of April.

Conclusion: An expense pertaining to a fiscal year must be accrued in the same year, regardless of when it was actually paid. If an expense pertaining to a fiscal year is not paid until the next fiscal year, it must be accrued as an expense and a payable at year-end.

Mortgage or Loan amortization: Method 1

Most small businesses and businesses in general need to take a mortgage or loan to sustain business operations. You pay a monthly amount mixed with Principle and interest. How do you record the loan Principle and how do you record the loan interest?

The easiest way is to make a loan amortization schedule. The bank can provide you with one or you can make one yourself. Generally, interest portion is higher at the beginning of the loan, and the Principle portion becomes higher towards the end of the loan.

Example.

Let's take a really simple example. Say you take a loan of $1,000, and the required monthly payment is $200. The bank gives you an amortization schedule as follows:

Monthly payment	Principle	Interest	Principle balance
			1,000
200	20	180	980
200	40	160	940
200	60	140	880
200	80	120	800
200	100	100	700
Total	300	700	

To record the loan of $1,000, the following is the journal entry:

Dr. Cash 1,000

Cr. Loan payable 1,000

To record loan payable.

There are two ways to record the monthly payments.

Example.

Method 1:

One way is to debit the loan payable and credit cash for the full amount of the monthly payment as follows:

Dr. Loan payable   200

   Cr. Cash   200

To record monthly payment on loan.

You would record this every month, and make an adjustment at quarter-end or year-end when you need to produce financial statements.

Example.
At the end of the five payments, Loan payable would have been debited 5 times, making the balance $0. However, as we can see from the table this is not reality, because the $200 payments include interest which does not decrease the balance of the loan. Therefore, the adjustment to record interest and adjust the Principle portion is:

Dr. Interest expense 700
  Cr. Loan payable   700
To adjust for interest expense on the loan.

Now, this brings the loan balance to the correct amount of $700 (agrees to the amortization schedule), and records interest expense of $700 on the income statement.

Mortgage or Loan amortization: Method 2

Example.

Method 2:
The second method is to record the Principle portion and interest portion separately each month. Here is the amortization schedule again for your convenience:

Monthly payment	Principle	Interest	Principle balance
			1,000
200	20	180	980
200	40	160	940
200	60	140	880
200	80	120	800
200	100	100	700
Total	300	700	

To record Principle and interest portions, the journal entry for the first payment would be:

Dr. Loan payable   20
Dr. Interest expense 180
   Cr. Cash   200
To record Principle and interest paid on the loan for the first month.

Example.

The second month would be similar, using the amounts from the table above:

Dr. Loan payable   40

Dr. Interest expense 160

  Cr. Cash   200

To record Principle and interest paid on the loan for the first month.

After doing the journal entries for the five months, the result of Method 2 would be the same as Method 1, with Loan payable at a $700 balance, and $700 recorded in the interest expense account.

Recording Amortization (Depreciation) of Tangible Capital Assets

This is an essential accounting concept that accountants and bookkeepers in most businesses must understand, but in my experience as a CPA most clients do not know how to properly record amortization of capital assets. It is a simple concept and quite easy to do once you know the basics.

Basic concept: Capital assets are assets that are useful for more than one year, and they must be depreciated over its useful life. For assets that are used up within one year, a business can expense the full amount within the year.

Why do we have to capitalize capital assets and amortize them over their useful life? Let's demonstrate with an example.

Example.

A business has net income of $1,000 every year. A computer with a cost of $1,500 is purchased and it is useful for 3 years.

Scenario 1.

If the computer is expensed fully in the year it is purchased, the business will have a net loss of $500 as follows:

Year 1:
Net income: $1,000 before computer purchase

    Computer purchase   (1,500)
    Net income   ($500)

Year 2:
Net income $1,000

Year 3:
Net income $1,000

This will cause huge variance in net income (a huge loss of $500) in the year of the computer purchase, with $1,000 net income in each of the two years to follow, assuming all other factors stay the same. If the computer was amortized over 3 years, each year's net income should be $500 ($1,000 net income minus $500 amortization each year). Year 1 income is UNDERSTATED by $1,000, while Year 2 & Year 3 are OVERSTATED by $500 each.

Principle: In accounting, there is a Principle called the Matching Principle, which calls for expenses to be matched to the year of the revenue earned. The computer is expected to earn revenue for 3 years, so the expense of purchasing the computer must be allocated over 3 years. This is called amortization (depreciation). This is done properly in the next scenario below.

Example.

Scenario 2.

The computer costing $1,500 is amortized over 3 years. Each year the amortization (depreciation) expense is $500 ($1,500 / 3).

Year 1, 2, and 3:

Net income: $1,000

Amortization: ($500)

Net income $500

Conclusion: There is no huge variance in income. Each year the net income after amortization is $500. This reflects the fact that the useful life of the computer is 3 years, and the computer is helping the business earn income in each of those 3 years, so the expense of purchasing the computer is spread out over the 3 years, fulfilling the Accounting Matching Principle.

Recording Term Deposits, and Interes Received from Term Deposits or GIC's

Many businesses when they become profitable put extra money into investments: term deposits, mutual funds, stocks, etc. In this section we will discuss how to record these investments and the related income generated.

Principle: Short term assets such as cash can be used within 1 year, so it is classified as a current asset (less than 1 year) on the balance sheet. But if the cash is invested in investments longer than 1 year, it must be classified as a long-term asset on the balance sheet, such as Investments.

If a business puts $1,000 into a 3-year term deposit, the following journal entry is required:

Example.

Dr. Investments $1,000   (long-term asset)

   Cr. Cash $1,000

To record investment in a 3-year term deposit.

Example.

Let's say $100 interest income is earned and it is deposited into the cash account. The interest earned on the term deposit will be recorded as follows:

Dr. Cash $100   (current asset)

   Cr. Interest income $100

To record interest income received on the term deposit.

Example.

How about if the $100 interest income is re-invested into the term deposit, and it cannot be withdrawn for the remainder of the 3 years? In this case, the Investment account should increase by $100 instead of the cash account.

Dr. Investment $100

   Cr. Interest income $100

To record interest income re-invested on the term deposit.

Recording Investments, Dividends & Interest Received from Investments

Sometimes businesses invest in the stock market. This is different from a term deposit in that there is a book value and a market value. Book value is how much was invested by the company. Market value is how much the stock is worth in the market.

Let's say a business invests $2,000 into the stock market and purchases shares of another company, Company A. The journal entry would be:

Dr. Investment $2,000

   Cr. Cash $2,000

To record investment in Company A.

Example.

If Company A issues a cash dividend of $200, the journal entry would be as follows:

Dr. Cash $200

   Cr. Dividend income $200

To record dividend income received.

Example.

If Company A issues a dividend that is re-invested into the investment, the journal entry would be as follows:

Dr. Investment $200

  Cr. Dividend income $200

To record dividend income re-invested on the investment.

Usually on the investment statement it would clearly say "Dividend" or "Re-invested dividend". Depending on whether the "Cash" account in the investment statement is affected, either one of the above examples are used.

Recording a Return of Capital from an Investment

Example.

What if Company A issues a $300 Return of Capital (ROC) on the investment? A return of capital is sometimes done when a company has excess assets and wants to return some of the capital invested by its investors to its investors. The journal entry is as follows:

Dr. Cash $300

   Cr. Investment $300

To record Return of Capital on Investment.

In this case, you will see "Return of Capital" or "ROC" on the investment statement.

Adjusting an Investment to Fair Market Value

Example.

Let's say a business invests $1,200 into shares of Company B. This is the "Book Value" of the shares.

Dr. Investment $1,200

　Cr. Cash $1,200

To record investment in Company B.

At the end of the year, an investment statement shows that the Fair Market Value of Company B shares owned by the business is $1,500. There is a difference between the Book Value of $1,200 and the Fair Market Value of $1,500.

Depending on the accounting policy of the business, one of two things can happen:

Example.

If the accounting policy is to keep investments at book value, this is simple. The business does not adjust the Investment to Fair Market Value. The Investment account remains at Book Value. Nothing needs to be done.

Example.

However, if the accounting policy is to write up or down to Fair Market Value, the following journal entry is required:

Dr. Investment $300

   Cr. Unrealized gain on investment $300

To record unrealized gain on investment in Company B.

Principle: The adjustment to Fair Market Value is an "Unrealized Gain" because the investment has not been sold yet. When the investment is sold, then the gain is realized.

Recording Dividend Payments to Shareholders

Sometimes a company pays a dividend to its shareholders. It's a way of distributing wealth that has accumulated inside the company back to its owners.

Let's say a company pays a $1,000 dividend to its owners. The journal entry would be:

Dr. Dividend   1,000

    Cr. Cash   1,000

To record dividend paid.

Closing Dividends into Retained Earnings

Normally, an expense account would be rolled into retained earnings at the end of the year. However, a dividend account is a Statement of Equity account. During the year-end close in an accounting software such as Quickbooks or Sage 50, the dividend account remains. What this means is that the opening retained earnings of the new year does not match the retained earnings of the previous year.

This is easy to fix. Whenever I start on a file for a client, one of the first things I do is to close out prior year dividends into retained earnings.

Example.

This is the journal entry to close out prior year dividends into retained earnings:

Dr. Retained earnings   1,000

　Cr. Dividend   1,000

To close prior year dividend into retained earnings.

That's it! Now your opening retained earnings agrees to prior year's closing retained earnings.

How to Determine Bad Debts Amounts (Uncollectible Accounts Receivable): Method 1

In an ideal world, all the customers of a business would pay their invoices. But the reality is that some customers either cannot pay the invoice or refuse to pay the invoice. When that happens, a bad debt occurs.

Most accounting software is able to produce a "Aged Accounts Receivable" report, which separates all the accounts receivable into "Current" (less than 30 days outstanding), 30-60 days, 60-90 days, and 90+ days.

When do you write off bad debts? It depends on your industry. In some industries customers usually pay within 30 days, and in that case, if you have many customer accounts that are outstanding for more than 30 days, you start to worry they will become bad debts. In some other industries, it is normal of customer to pay within 60 days. So you wouldn't worry as much until the customer accounts become outstanding for more than 60 days.

In most cases, if the amount your customers owe you become outstanding for more than 90+ days, there is a high chance they will become bad debts. These are amounts owed to you by your customers that you are unlikely able to collect. The exception is if you have a financing agreement with your customer to pay at a scheduled time and frequency. If you don't have such a financing agreement in place, you probably will have some bad debts.

One way to determine the amount of bad debts or the amount for setting up Allowance for Doubtful Accounts is to use the percentage method.

Example.

Let's say your Accounts Receivable has the following amounts:

<30 days outstanding	30-60 days	60-90 days	90+ days outstanding
$500	$300	$200	$100

Based on your previous experience or using industry percentages, you may decide to use the following percentages for bad debts/Allowance for Doubtful Accounts:

	<30 days outstanding	30-60 days	60-90 days	90+ days outstanding
	$500	$300	$200	$100
	0%	10%	20%	50%
Bad debts	$0	$30	$40	$50

The longer an amount is outstanding, the less likely payment will be collected from the customer. Therefore, the percentage of bad debts is typically higher going from less than 30 days to 30-60 days to 60-90 days to 90+ days. You simply multiply the amount by the percentage you assign. Then you do the journal entries described in the next section.

How to Determine Bad Debts Amounts (Uncollectible Accounts Receivable): Method 2

Example.

Another method to determine bad debts/Allowance for Doubtful Accounts is to look at each customer account, and based on your previous dealings with the customer or your knowledge of their financial situation, decide which accounts to write-off as bad debt or set up an Allowance for Doubtful Account.

Customer	Days outstanding	Amount	Collectible?
Customer A	90+	$20	No, write-off as bad debt
Customer B	90+	$30	No, write-off as bad debt
Customer C	90+	$25	Yes, expecting their big customer to pay soon
Customer D	90+	$25	Yes, slow payer but will pay

In this case, the $20 and $30 amount will be written off as bad debt or an Allowance for Doubtful Accounts will be set up for Customer A and Customer B. Since management believes Customers C and D will eventually pay, the Accounts Receivable amount is left intact on the balance sheet.

Writing-off Bad Debts

Example.

Let's say you print out your "Aged Accounts Receivable Report", and decide some customers are not likely to pay you and the total amount uncollectible is $300. What do you do?

Method 1: Allowance for bad debts

This method allows you to adjust the accounts that you think are uncollectible, without impacting your income statement and net income.

Dr. Allowance for bad debts   300   (Balance sheet account)

   Cr. Accounts receivable   300

To record allowance for doubtful accounts.

Notice that this "Allowance for Bad Debts" account is a balance sheet account, so it does not lower your net income on the income statement the way a bad debt expense would do, as will be described in Method 2 below.

Example.

Method 2: Directly write-off bad debts

Using the same example above, you think $300 of your accounts receivable is uncollectible.

Dr. Bad debts expense   300   (Income statement account)

Cr. Accounts receivable   300

To write-off bad debts expense.

This method of directly writing off bad-debts completely removes them from the balance sheet, and increases expense by $300 and net income decreases by $300.

Setting up Allowance for Doubtful Accounts

You can also combine Method 1 & Method 2 by writing off some bad debts expense and setting up others by using Allowance for bad debts.

Example.

But what if after you write off an account as bad debt, and the customer suddenly one day pays you? It's simple if you use Method 1. First, you have to reverse your Allowance for Doubtful Accounts:

Dr. Accounts receivable   300

   Cr. Allowance for doubtful accounts   300

To reverse allowance for doubtful accounts for payment received.

Example.

Next, you use this journal entry to record collection on cash:

Dr. Cash   300

   Cr. Accounts receivable

To record payment received on accounts receivable.

Example.

If you had used Method 2, the accounts receivable has already been completely written off. You would then record as follows:

Dr. Cash   300

  Cr. Revenue   300

To record payment received from customer.

Using this method the net effect is zero. Your expense increased the previous year, and your revenue increased this year. Net income would look more volatile, so it may be better to use the Allowance for Doubtful Accounts method so that net income doesn't fluctuate from year-to-year.

Setting up Accounting Software

I will use the popular accounting software for small & medium sized businesses, Sage 50 (previously known as Simply Accounting) for demonstration. However, it's very similar for Quickbooks, ACCPAC, and other accounting software.

Bookkeeping: Sage 50, Simply Accounting Basics

I entered the accounting profession in 2007. I remember the first task given to me was to do bank reconciliations for a year for a hair salon. After that, I was to enter all the transactions into Simply Accounting (now called Sage 50). The client that I recently visited, was using Sage 50 as the accounting software.

Sage 50 is designed to be user friendly and easy to use. It is designed for people who do not have extensive accounting training. I have used both Simply Accounting (now Sage 50) and Quickbooks, the two most popular off-the-shelf accounting software packages. They are similar in many ways, but also different in many other ways.

Some people prefer Simply Accounting (now Sage 50), and other people prefer Quickbooks. It's all a matter of preference. I find them both quite easy to use.

About half of our clients use Simply Accounting (now Sage 50), and the other half use Quickbooks. A small portion use other accounting software such as MYOB, ACCPAC, Great Plains, etc.

Getting Started with Accounting Software

Sage 50 is designed for smaller and medium sized and home businesses. It is designed to be purchased off the shelf, easy to install, easy to set up for your business, and start using right away.

There are several versions of this Sage 50 software, including Sage 50 Pro Accounting, Sage 50 Premium Accounting, and Sage 50 Quantum Accounting. For a small local business, the most basic accounting package will do nicely.

The Home Window is where you will be spending a lot of time. Most businesses will use the Customer & Sales (for Sales Invoices, Receipts), and Vendors & Purchases sections. You may also choose to use the Employees & Payroll function, or outsource it to a reputable payroll company.

On the right side of the Customers & Sales screen you will see a list of customers and their contact information as well as their balance owing. This is very useful because the livelihood of a business depends on its customers ability to pay on a reasonable time frame. As I discussed in my books "Bookkeeping & Accounting Basics For Small Business & Home Business" and "Understanding Financial Statement Analysis", a company with a lot of revenue can still be in a lot of financial trouble if it does not collect money from its customers.

Even if a company has a lot of revenue and sales, it must be able to pay its own bills such as rent, utilities, payroll, and other operating expenses. If the company does not collect cash from its customers and only rely on credit sales, the company could be in financial distress despite a healthy looking sales/revenue line on its income statement.

If you are ever lost using Sage 50, you can refer to eBooks such as this one, or make use of the Sage Online Community. I've never used this myself, but it could be another resource you can use.

To create a profile for your company in Sage 50, you will need to know the first day of your fiscal year as well as the fiscal year end. Most businesses will have January 1 as their fiscal year beginning, and December 31 as their fiscal year end.

If you are not sure about your fiscal year starts and end dates, you can consult your external accountants or your lawyer who helped you with your incorporation.

Trial Balance

A trial balance is one of the most important pieces of information for accountants like me. Whenever I start on a new year end file for a client, I ask for a trial balance.

A trial balance is simply a list of all your account balances at a particular time. The trial balance will list all of your account balances such as assets, liabilities, equity, revenue, and expenses.

Creating a New Company

If you are converting from Quickbooks, there is the Quickbooks conversion option. The wizard will show you how to do it.

If you are creating a company from scratch, you will need to enter your company name and address information. You will enter your fiscal year starts date, the earliest transaction date which is usually the fiscal year start date, as well as the fiscal year end date.

Next select your industry. Sage 50 will create accounts that are specific to your industry. For example, if you are a manufacturing company, Sage 50 will create inventory accounts for you. If you are in the service industry, Sage 50 will tailor the accounts to your specific industry.

Follow the wizard to finish setting up your company.

You may want to set up the sales taxes function. This will lets you select the appropriate tax rates for your federal, state, or provincial taxes. If you use foreign currencies, Sage 50 has functions that can help you track those foreign currencies.

Report and Form Options

I highly recommend you experiment with the settings. Different businesses need different reports. You may find some reports that give you exactly the financial information you need from Sage 50.

Account names and account numbers

Accounts numbers go in this order:
Assets: 1000 - 1999
Liabilities: 2000 - 2999
Equity: 3000 - 3999
Revenue: 4000 - 4999
Expenses: 5000 - 5999

Most accounting firms will use similar account groupings. It is best to stay with these groupings so things are consistent from the bookkeeping to the year-end financial statements and tax return preparations.

Sage 50 also decide accounts into different account types.

H = Group Heading. For example, Current Assets. Current assets is actually not a transaction account. Current assets include cash, accounts receivable, and inventories.

A = Subgroup Account. Subgroup accounts are used in transactions.

S = Subtotal. Subtotal is the total off all subgroup accounts on the account list. Subtotal is not used for transactions.

G = Group Account. This is an account not part of a subtotal. Group Accounts are used in transactions.

T = Group Total. Group Total is total of subtotals and group accounts. A Group Total is not a transaction account.

Account Class

There are different account classes in Sage 50. For example, bank is an account class. Simply select the appropriate fields and fill in the banking information such as bank name, branch name, transit number, and account number.

If you have been in business for a while, you will have to enter the existing balances into Sage 50. If you are starting a new business, then you will start with no previous transactions or account balances.

To check your account balances at anytime, you should run a trial balance report.

Customers & Vendors Setup

At the heart of every business is the customers and vendors. No business can survive without customers or vendors. Start by entering customer information.

1. Enter the customer's name
2. Ensure their contact and address
3. Enter any customer balances

Note you can import customer information from Quickbooks, Quicken, or MYOB using the Sage 50 Import Wizard.

Final thoughts

I hope you've found this book useful and can keep it at your desk as a quick reference tool. You can search Amazon for "Calvin K Lee" for my other books. You will find them inspirational and improve the quality of your life.

To thank you for getting this book, you can get another FREE eBook on my website:
www.hellocalvinlee.com/free-ebook

To learn more about bookkeeping and accounting, you can read my book "Bookkeeping & Accounting Basics for Small Business & Home Business".

If you want to learn more about understanding Financial Statement Analysis, my book on this topic may interest you: Understanding Financial Statement Analysis: For Accountants, Business Owners, Investors, and Stakeholders.

Join my Facebook author fan page for new books:
https://www.facebook.com/hellocalvinlee/

Click here to go to my Amazon author page with all my books.

If you enjoyed this book, please go to Amazon's website and rate my book. It takes a minute to rate the number of stars and it will help other readers see that you enjoyed my book and so they can also benefit from it. Please also leave a comment on what you enjoyed most from the book. Leaving a comment is optional, but will be really helpful for my books to attract more readers so more people can benefit. I appreciate your assistance!

About the Author

Calvin K. Lee, MBA, CPA, CA, CPA (Illinois) is an accountant, author, composer, and teacher. He has lived in Beijing, Hong Kong, Toronto, and Vancouver, and travelled to many countries including the U.S.; to Europe such as the U.K., France, Italy, Germany, and Switzerland; and to Asia such as China, Malaysia, Singapore, Japan, and Thailand. Some of his favorite topics include love, relationships, effective communication, psychology, leadership, teamwork, and business. His biggest passion is inspiring and helping others achieve their goals. To do this, Calvin has been writing articles for his blog for over 10 years to inspire and encourage others.

Calvin holds an undergraduate degree from the University of British Columbia in Vancouver, a MBA degree with distinction from York University in Toronto, Canada and a Double MBA degree from Peking University in Beijing, China in 2016. He is a CPA designated accountant in the U.S. and Canada, and also a CPA and Chartered Accountant in Canada. In addition to his successful career in accounting, he has also taught Master of Accounting classes at university, taught accounting modules at the CPA professional association, and enjoys being a mentor to younger accountants. He has served as President of the MBA Ambassadors during his MBA studies and as Chair of the Young Professionals Forum at the CPA Association.

Note to the reader

This book is written for general guidance, and is not a substitute for accounting, legal, tax, or other professional advice with a qualified advisor. Laws are always changing. While every effort is made to make this book current, there may be errors or omissions. This book is made available with no representations or warranties of any kind for the accuracy or completeness of this book. The author and/or publisher do not assume and hereby disclaim any liability or responsibility for any action or decision leading to claims, losses or damages by any person(s) relying on the contents of this book. Consult a professional advisor as needed as the examples may or may not be applicable to your situation. The accounting standards discussed here follows standards pertaining to small & medium sized enterprises. While these bookkeeping & accounting concepts can be similar in other parts of the world, there may be some differences.

Contact the author

Website: www.hellocalvinlee.com

Podcast: www.hellocalvinlee.com/podcast

Amazon page:
www.amazon.com/author/hellocalvinlee

Blog: www.hellocalvinlee.com/blog
https://calvinklee2010.wordpress.com/

Facebook page:
https://www.facebook.com/hellocalvinlee

E-mail: hellocalvinlee@gmail.com

Twitter: @calvinklee2010
www.Twitter.com/calvinklee2010

If there are any topics you want me to write about in a future book, I'd love to know!

I welcome feedback and comments.

Books by Calvin K. Lee

1. How to Increase Confidence and Succeed in Meeting People

2. Living an Extraordinary and Amazingly Purposeful Life: 9 Principles to a Better Life

3. Words of Wisdom, Encouragement, and Inspiration: Bring Happiness into Your Life

4. How to Work Smarter, Not Harder: Success in the Workplace

5. A Collection of Short Stories: And the Moral of the Story is…?

6. *Bookkeeping and Accounting Basics for Small & Medium Sized Businesses and Home Businesses: Over 20 Examples of Common Accounting Transactions!* ***ACCOUNTING & BOOKKEEPING***

7. *Understanding Financial Statements: For Accountants, Business Owners, Investors, and Stakeholders* ***ACCOUNTING & BOOKKEEPING***

8. LEAP before you THINK

9. TIME MANAGEMENT: saving 4 HOURS a week

10. From Ordinary to Extraordinary: How God Used Ordinary Men and Women in the Bible

11. How to Get Out of Debt

*12. **Bookkeeping & Accounting Explained for Small Business & Home Business the Easy Way (Over 25+ Examples) ***ACCOUNTING & BOOKKEEPING******

BONUS book #1:

"How to Increase Confidence and Succeed in Meeting People: Business Networking the Easy Way...Meet New People Now!"

©2015 Calvin Lee
All rights reserved

This book or any portion thereof may not be reproduced or used without written permission of the author/publisher except in brief quotations, book reviews, and articles.

How to Increase Confidence and Succeed in Meeting People: Business Networking the Easy Way

Meet New People Now!
CALVIN K. LEE, MBA

Bookkeeping & Accounting Explained

How to Increase Confidence and Succeed in Meeting People: Business Networking the Easy Way...Meet New People Now!

Calvin K. Lee, MBA, CPA, CA, CPA (Illinois)

©2015 Calvin Lee
All rights reserved

This book or any portion thereof may not be reproduced or used without written permission of the author/publisher except in brief quotations, book reviews, and articles.

ISBN-13: 978-1522777977

ISBN-10: 1522777970

Praise from readers

"Good read. Networking is so important at work, church and even personal life. How can we take charge and embrace it? Very practical, good reading!"

- V.C.

"By using his own example, Calvin gives hope for the readers."

- J.L.

"Five stars. Great real life experience that you can relate to easily."

- D.L.

Table of Contents

1. Does networking make you scared?

2. Defining networking

3. Can introverts become good at networking?

4. The benefit of networking

5. Networking like a pro

6. You never know who knows who!

7. Maintaining your network

CONCLUSION

1. Does networking make you scared?

Networking...

Did you shudder just hearing that word? Does networking give you the chills? Are you afraid of not knowing what to say and facing the awkward silence?

Fear not, my friend. I was once in your position. In fact, when I was in elementary school, I was so shy that one of my few friends said to me during an Andy Warhol art exhibit field trip: "Calvin, you don't have any friends." Ouch. I still remember that day clearly. He said it while we were near the top of the escalator.

In high school, I wasn't very popular either. I always envied people who were naturally outgoing, serving on student council, having lots of friends, going to parties, etc. I wasn't invited to many parties.

In university I remember one day I was walking around thinking, why do I fear being around other people? Why do I have to keep wearing this mask of confidence? Why can't I just be myself? Why can't I naturally be like those outgoing people to whom talking and socializing (gulp) comes so easily?

Fast forward to today, I have grasped the basics of networking, and a lot of people ask me how I do networking so easily. One of my professors saw me networking with my classmates before class and said, "Calvin, you're a social butterfly!" I get invited to a lot of events, and am still having fun meeting new people.

This is a short book on how I went from dreading networking to embracing it. And with some effort, you can do it too. If I can do it, you can do it.

2. Defining networking

I define networking as meeting people you don't know with the purpose of making more friends, business contacts, and building professional networks.

Networking does not mean hanging out with the people you know all the time.

Networking isn't one of those things you can learn completely out of a book. It's like learning to ride a bicycle. Sure you'll be wobbly at first, but it's interesting that to maintain balance you can't stand still. You have to move and create momentum in order to stay balanced on a bicycle. It's the same with networking. You can't stand still and not go talk to someone. You have to get out of your comfort zone and just say, "Hi." You have to throw yourself out there and trust you will survive.

If I can do it, you can do it too.

I've met resistance from people when I tell them about the benefits of networking. They would argue that close friends and connections are enough. While having close friends are important, people who are not used to networking cannot understand the tremendous value of networking because they have never done it and have never seen the amazing results that come from networking.

People who like to stay in their own comfort zone with their close group of friends do not understand the power of "Weak ties". Weak ties are the people you see just occasionally in a year, maybe once or twice a year, and you don't see them on a regular basis. When it comes to finding a job, it is well documented by other authors and articles on LinkedIn that "Weak ties" have tremendous potential to helping you with your career. This is because your close group of friends likely has the same circle of people as you. This really limits the amount of people you and your close friends know. However, "Weak ties" are generally outside your close circle of friends and so the number of people they know can be quite significant.

3. Can introverts become good at networking?

I expect some readers of this book are introverts. You hate networking. Extroverts by nature get energized when they are around people, so they tend to naturally like networking (socializing).

There are differences between introverts and extroverts. If you are an introvert, you could only be successful for a while at pretending to be an extrovert before you run out of energy and need to rest for a few days. That's right – if you push yourself to be an extrovert, you may need to go hide and rest for days.

First, you need to know being shy and needing solitude are two completely separate things. If you're an introvert, that's not going to change. You still need your solitude times to regenerate your energy when you're alone. However, you can overcome your shyness and can get out there and meet people.

There are many famous introverts: Abraham Lincoln and Bill Gates are just two examples.

I believe introverts can grow into ambiverts. Ambiverts are people who can use characteristics from both introverts and extroverts. It's a matter of practice being brave. You can become an ambivert by practicing networking skills.

4. The benefit of networking

You probably already know the benefits of networking, or if you don't, a simple Google search would give you hundreds if not thousands of results. I will point out main benefit of networking that I find most useful myself.

Benefit: Networking is great for looking for a job.

People say most jobs are never advertised. The hiring manager will first ask his or her staff if they know anybody who can fill the position. Then the hiring manager may ask other departments to see if any internal candidates or people the staff know can fill the position. This all happens before the job is posted, and by this point, many jobs are already filled. That's why you want to network and try to get this inside information.

5. Networking like a pro

When I attend an event, I aim to start my networking at the top. Every event has limited time, and you have limited energy. You want the best bang for your buck. What I mean by starting at the top is to meet the organizers of an event. They will likely be wandering around the room with an officially looking nametag that is computer printed with a nice company logo, while the other participants are all wearing sticker nametags.

Why should you start with the organizers of an event? They can easily introduce you to other people. They will likely know a lot of people in the room, and they can introduce you to other members of the organizing committee. In other words, they are a great resource to start.

It's also easy to start a conversation with the organizers. You already know a lot about them. They organized the event. You can tell them they organized a great event, ask them how long it took to organize, how many guests are expected to come, etc.

Don't worry so much about your own performance. If you focus and enjoy what the other person is saying, it takes a lot of pressure of you. People love to talk about themselves. Once you learn how to get people to talk about themselves, just open both ears and listen!

6. You never know who knows who!

I network with everyone, with people above my level, people at the same level as me, and people below my level. Yes, even with people I consider below my level. The rationale is simple: you never know who knows who! That administrative assistant may just know a CEO or manager who's currently hiring. They have that information that you don't have! The point is you never know who knows who. That's why while you should focus on certain groups of people to network with, don't neglect to network with people who seem outside of your circle.

The more you network, the easier it becomes. The first time you go networking, you may not know anyone. As I'm writing this I attended a new networking event for me this morning that I only knew one person. By the end of the event, I knew nearly 20 people. Next time I come back to a similar event, I'll probably meet a few people I've met already today. As you can see, networking can be fun!

7. Maintaining your network

The longer it takes you to re-establish contact with a person the less useful that connection will be to you when you need to use your network. I recommend you contact important people in your network on at least an annual basis. It's simple if you use LinkedIn. LinkedIn has a feature in which it e-mails you when a connection has a work anniversary or a new job. That's the best time to send them an e-mail and say congratulations.

Here's a sample on how you can use an e-mail to congratulate a connection on their new job or work anniversary:

Hi Bob,

LinkedIn sent me a message that you're celebrating 8 years working at ABC Bank! Congratulations!

I've just celebrated 3 years working at XYZ Company myself this past April.

Best Regards,

Calvin

I usually try to mention something about how I'm doing so my contact has something to talk about. As well, it keeps them in the loop on how your career is doing.

Join my Facebook author fan page for new books:
https://www.facebook.com/hellocalvinlee/

CONCLUSION

Well, there you have it. I have given you many networking tips and advice I've learned by trial-and-error. Now all that's left to do is for you to get out there, and immerse yourself with networking. Start small, set a goal of talking to 1-2 people whom you don't know. If you're adventurous, start with 5 people like I did. The benefits are numerous. Most of all have fun. You'll enjoy the journey a lot more!

Happy networking!

I hope you've found this book useful and can keep it at your desk as a quick reference tool.

For more free content, visit www.hellocalvinlee.com

Bookkeeping & Accounting Explained

BONUS book #2:

"Living an Extraordinary and Amazingly Purposeful Life: 9 Principles to a Better Life"

©2015 Calvin Lee
All rights reserved

This book or any portion thereof may not be reproduced or used without written permission of the author/publisher except in brief quotations, book reviews, and articles.

Bookkeeping & Accounting Explained

Living an Extraordinary and Amazingly Purposeful Life

9 Principles to a Better Life

Calvin K. Lee, MBA, CPA

Bookkeeping & Accounting Explained

Living an Extraordinary and Amazing Purposeful Life: 9 Principles to Live a Better Life

Calvin K. Lee, MBA, CPA

©2015

All Rights Reserved

Dedicated to my parents and brother:

You have always encouraged and supported me in everything I do, so that I can live an extraordinary and amazingly purposeful life.

Table of Contents

Introduction

1. How do I step out of my comfort zone?
2. What are you thinking?
3. Be yourself
4. Know yourself
5. Don't let other people run your life
6. Set a S.M.A.R.T. goal!
7. Take risks!
8. Who do you want as friends?
9. Continuous learning

Introduction

Most people want to live an extraordinary life, but not everybody who wants to does.

With effort, I believe everyone and everybody who wants to live an extraordinary life can. In my own life, I've lived in four different cities, met hundreds of people from all over the world, and enjoy a career that I love. I consider my life extraordinary even though I am just a very normal, average person growing up in a normal, average household. The key is the attitude of the mind, as well as taking appropriate action.

Turn the page and let the journey begin!

1. How do I step out of my comfort zone?

People love their comfort zone. That's why they don't live extraordinary lives.

First of all, you have to have a deep desire for a better life, and you'll do anything to get it. And that means some temporary discomfort. People get bored of routine. You work the same job every day, but you don't change. The most likely reason is the current job is comfortable.

What I've found in my own journey is the decision to step out is the most difficult part. I remember going to zip line some years ago, where there is a wire hanging between two high poles with the rider strapped into a harness and fly across the two poles at a very fast speed.

We were required to climb up a really tall pole, the height of an electric cable pole, two or three stories high. As someone who is afraid of heights, climbing up the pole was scary, I had to remind myself to not look down. But climbing wasn't the scariest part. I remember there was a small platform at the top to sit on, the moment before you jump. I was horrified, petrified, mortified. I remember thinking to myself, "What did I get myself into?" After a few seconds of hesitation, which felt like eternity, I leaped off the platform, and had the thrill of my life zip lining. Once I made the jump, I was no longer afraid.

> **KEY POINT: To live an extraordinary and amazing life...You have to jump and take a leap of faith!**

What does this mean in real life?

Several years ago I remember joining a volunteer committee for my profession to organize educational & social events for young professionals. I was a committee member and one day, the chairperson announced she was stepping down, and asked for volunteers to take over her role. I was excited at the opportunity, but I also had my doubts. Fear and worries flooded my mind:

Who am I to take this role? Do I have what it takes?

I don't have the experience.

What if I don't do a good job?

Knowing that the longer I hesitate the more worries and excuses my mind will come up with, I decided to take a leap of faith and just raise my hand and volunteer. The rest is history.

PUT IT INTO PRACTICE: Try to step out of your comfort zone a little everyday. That way, when a big decision comes up, you'll be more ready to take the leap of faith.

Do this, and you're well on your way to an extraordinary life!

2. What are you thinking?
How you think affects what you do.

Henry Ford said, "If you think you can, or if you think you can't, you're right."

You are a result of your thoughts. If you think you can't succeed at something, you probably won't. Even if you try, you'll just get in your own way to sabotage your chance of success, or bail out at the first problem you encounter.

If you think you can do it, and have the persistence to do it, you'll have a better chance at succeeding than if you think you can't do it.

Always be aware of what you are thinking. As soon as you find yourself thinking of a negative thought, get rid of it like a hot potato!

If you keep thinking of a negative thought, you'll keep thinking about it. If you try *not* to think about a negative thought, you'll also keep thinking about it! Imagine if I ask you to not think about a rabbit. What do you think of? A rabbit! We think about what we try not to think about.

Therefore, the way to get rid of a thought you don't want is to find a **replacement** thought for it. Our minds cannot think of two things at the same time. Once you start thinking about something else, it replaces the old thought.

Starting today, instead of thinking of what you can't do, think of what you *can* do. This allows your creativity to work in your favor and figure out new ways to do things that you previously thought were impossible.

PUT IT INTO ACTION: Think of what you can do, rather than what you can't do. If there is something you can't do, find a way to get around it so you can achieve your goal. Believe you can do it.

3. Be yourself

This is one of the hardest lessons I've had to learn. Many people wear a mask around other people, concealing their fears, weaknesses, and vulnerabilities. I've read Donald Miller's best selling book "*Scary Close*", where he talks about opening up to people and how liberating it feels to be known.

One of the biggest tragedies in life is being on your deathbed surrounded by people who love you but didn't really know you. Deep down inside, all of us have a deep craving to be known by those we love.

It was very hard at first, but I've learned that vulnerabilities and weaknesses is what connects me to other people. Holding up an image of having everything together all the time can be very fatiguing. Besides, no one in life has everything together at all times. We all have struggles, problems, and failures. That doesn't mean you have to expose everything about yourself to everyone you meet. But during appropriate times and with the right people, it may be the most loving thing to do.

KEY POINT: practicing being yourself. Let your guard down and be willing to share your true thoughts.

When most people are asked, "How are you doing?" Most people will answer, "Fine." But reality is their life is a mess, their career is on the line, or their marriage is about to crumble. While it's not wise to share everything with everybody, do take time to share with the people that love you the most.

Remember, deep down inside people have a craving to be known.

PUT IT INTO ACTION: Next time when somebody asks you about yourself, instead of giving pre-programmed answers, try to give genuine true responses. Allow people to see the real you, not someone whom you think others would like.

It is better to be loved for who you are, rather than be loved for a version of you that you portray to others rather than the real you.

4. Know yourself

I know this section title sounds weird. You are with yourself 24/7, so how could you not know yourself?

I recently took a detailed career assessment test. I thought I knew myself and my needs and wants in my life and career, but my one hour consulting session with a trained consultant revealed things about myself that I either felt but could not put into words, or I didn't even realize about myself. It was quite an enlightening talk.

PUT IT INTO ACTION: One easy to get to know yourself from a 360-degree view is to ask other people: (1) What are my strengths? (2) What are my weaknesses?

I once asked several close family members and friends what they think are my strengths and weaknesses. The strengths were obvious as I knew them myself.

What shocked me was four out of five people told me a weakness I had no idea I had.

We can literally spend our whole lives learning about ourselves. Sometimes we have a blind spot that only other people can see. For example, some people have annoying habits they don't realize but their spouse, family, and everyone else knows about. The only person that doesn't know is the perpetrator himself or herself.

KEY POINT: Routinely ask people what they think about you. You may learn a lot about yourself you never knew about!

5. Don't let other people run your life

There was a man who became a doctor. But the day he became a doctor, he quit.

What happened? Many people dream of becoming a doctor for the prestige and high income. But for this man, he did it just to satisfy his parents. He didn't want to be a doctor. He wanted to be a chef.

KEY POINT: Listen to the advice of the people around you, but you have to make the decisions for yourself.

Stay true to yourself. This is really the only way to live an extraordinary life. If you are living the life someone else expects of you, you will be miserable.

PUT IT INTO ACTION: Is there a fire of passion burning inside of you that has yet to be realized? YOLO - You only live once. Follow your dreams and passions, and make your dreams into reality.

6. Set a S.M.A.R.T. goal!

So often people set goals but don't attain them. For a real life example, just go to your local gym and observe for 3-months starting in January. I've seen this happen before, where in January the number of people signing up for gym membership spikes, and the gym is really crowded with people with their New Year's Resolution to stay in shape. However, the number of people that perseveres through February dwindles, and in March only the really dedicated gym goers remain.

What's the problem?

The problem is people don't set goals that work.

I like the S.M.A.R.T. method of setting goals. I will do a brief overview here, and you can do a Google search and you'll find articles about this method in more detail.

S = Specific

M = Measurable

A = Attainable

R = Realistic

T = Timely

Your goal has to be **specific**, meaning you can't just say "My goal is to lose weight." It just doesn't work. You have to say, "My goal is to lose 5 pounds by the end of next month."

Next, it has to be **measurable**. In the example above, 5 pounds can be measured by a scale, and the calendar can tell when time is up.

Attainable goals mean the goal should be achievable. **Realistic** means the goal can be achieved within the time frame.

Finally, each goal should be **timely**. Not setting a deadline for yourself usually means that goal won't be worked on diligently enough to be achieved.

7. Take risks!

Sometimes I make decisions based on the question, "Would I regret it if I did **not** take this opportunity to...?" A study of staff at nursing homes have shown many dying patients regret what they did **not** do in their lives rather than what they did. Often, we are held back by fear. Fear of rejection, fear of the unknown, fear of failure.

I remember when I was in university I joined the ballroom dancing club. There was a dance competition coming up and there was a pretty girl in the dance club I wanted to partner with. The problem was I was scared to ask her to be my partner. I remember the dance club was held on the 2nd floor of the Student Union Building. I went downstairs and paced back and forth as I tried to muster enough courage to ask her to be my dance partner. I must have looked like an idiot walking back and forth in the same place!

Finally, I mustered enough courage and went back upstairs to ask her. She said, "Yes"! I was so happy I was jumping up and down (in my imagination of course!) All I said to her was, "Great."

I felt most alive when I was doing things I thought I wasn't capable of. The human body and mind are very interesting. They can grow and stretch beyond what we think is possible.

PUT IT INTO PRACTICE: Go ahead! Ask that pretty girl for a date. Go and live in a foreign country. Start your own business. Have an opinion that differs from other people and follow through to make positive impact and change.

You never know you can do it until you've tried. Don't be one of those people who regrets the things he or she did not do in their life.

KEY POINT: Take risks. You'll thank yourself later for being brave.

8. Who do you want as friends?

We become the average of the five people we spend the most time with. Over time, our thinking, values, habits become similar to those five people.

If you hang out with negative people, soon you'll feel negative too. Misery loves company. If you are around positive people, you will start to feel more positive. If you are around people who play it safe, you'll play it safe. If you are around people who know how to take calculated risks like starting a business, you might start a business yourself.

KEY POINT: If you want to live an extraordinary life, think about whether the people around you are living extraordinary lives. If they are, they will encourage you to live an extraordinary life. If you spend time with people who don't like change, over time you'll be more resistant to change. If you spend time with adventurous people, you are likely to become more adventurous.

PUT IT INTO ACTION: You may want to enlarge your circle of friends to find a supporting network to accommodate your dreams. You don't have to cut ties with your existing friends, but just remember who you spend the most time with have major influences on your thinking.

9. Continuous learning

I've heard many times people say after their last exam in university, "I'm so glad I'm done with school!"

Congratulations. You did it. You got your degree, diploma or certificate. That is worth celebrating.

But this is only the end of your formal education training. You graduate from the academic university, and now you enter the university of life and the university of society.

KEY POINT: Don't let your graduation day be the last day of learning! Be proactive and do lifelong learning.

People who live extraordinary lives are dedicated to lifelong learning. They realize the more they learn, the more they don't know. This is certainly true for me.

There are many ways to learn. I enjoy reading books, and I read on average 2 books a month which equals 24 books a year. I always think $10 or $15 for a book is well worth the investment, especially for young people but is true for any age. This is because someone who is an expert in the topic you read or who has experienced something is now writing the best parts and sharing it with you. It lets me avoid the pains the author had to go through to gain that experience!

For example, I love reading books on human relationships and communications. I've seen quite a few authors write, for example, about marriage, "I wish someone would have told me the things I write in this book when I was younger." Reading books lets you learn from someone else's experiences. But I know for many people reading books are boring.

PUT IT INTO PRACTICE: If you like reading books, great. But reading books is not your only learning option. You can listen to audio books. Listen while you're on your commute, when you're in the gym, when you're taking a stroll in the park. Audio books work well for some people and is a great time saver, while you stimulate the mind and learn new things.

You can also go to seminars, conferences, or take an evening or weekend class. Look at your local community college catalog and I'm sure you can find something that excites you, ranging from photography to business to dancing classes.

Final thoughts

No matter what background you come from, no matter what your past, no matter what has happened or what situation you're in, living an extraordinary life begins *today*. It begins with a decision to live purposefully, to grab life by the horns, and take responsibility for your own life. Don't wait for life to become better, don't wait for the right time. Act now.

To start, I encourage you to pick one or two principles to work on in your life. After you are comfortable applying one or two principles, pick an addition principle to work on.

Good luck!

If you enjoyed this book, please take a minute to rate it on Amazon's website. Your good rating will encourage me to write more great books. I appreciate it very much! ☺

BONUS book #3:

"Words of Wisdom, Encouragement, and Inspiration"

©2015 Calvin Lee
All rights reserved

This book or any portion thereof may not be reproduced or used without written permission of the author/publisher except in brief quotations, book reviews, and articles.

Calvin K. Lee, MBA, CPA
WORDS OF WISDOM, ENCOURAGEMENT, AND INSPIRATION (BOOK #3)

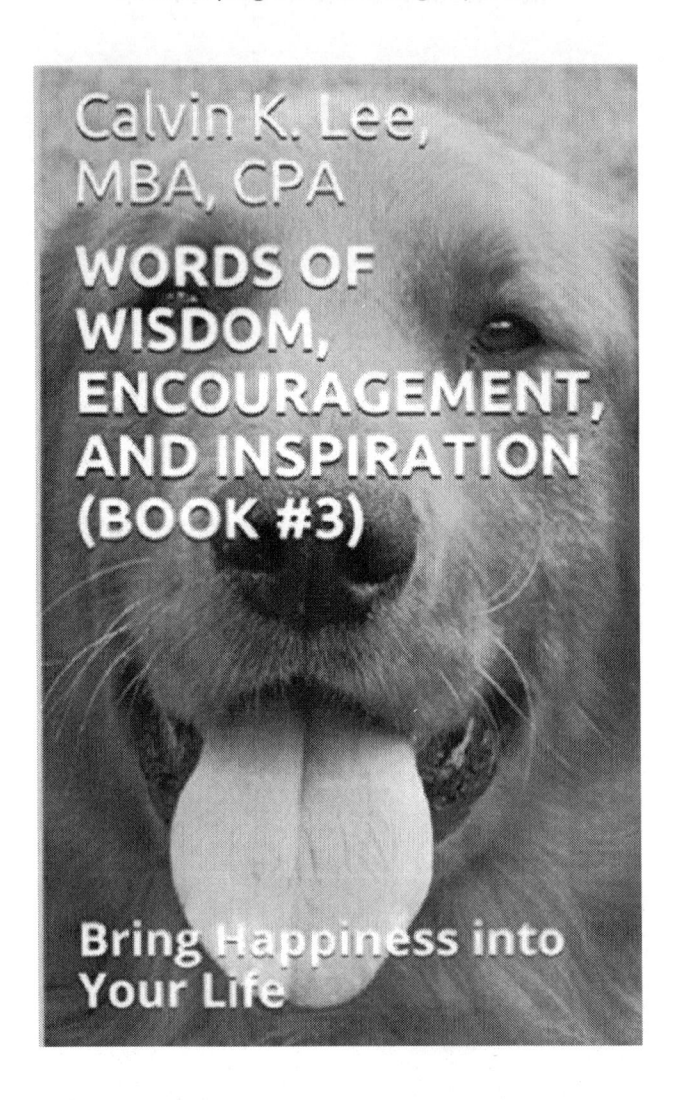

Bring Happiness into Your Life

Table of Contents

Introduction

1. How to be successful

2. Be thankful

3. Words of encouragement in pain and suffering

4. A brighter day will surely come

5. Words of wisdom on love

6. You are unique!

7. Fake it till you make it!

8. More words of wisdom

Note to the reader

This book is written for general guidance, and is not a substitute for accounting, legal, tax, or other professional advice with a qualified advisor. Laws are always changing. While every effort is made to make this book current, there may be errors or omissions. This book is made available with no representations or warranties of any kind for the accuracy or completeness of this book. The author and/or publisher do not assume and hereby disclaim any liability or responsibility for any action or decision leading to claims, losses or damages by any person(s) relying on the contents of this book. Consult a professional advisor as needed as the examples may or may not be applicable to your situation.

Praise from readers for Calvin's books:

"Very practical, good reading!"

"I really enjoy your books."

"Well done, very informative. I like how you used your example."

"By using his own example, Calvin gives hope for the readers."

"Great real life experience that you can relate to easily."

"Very clear, concise, and concrete. Well done."

"Practical tips and relatable examples. A pleasant read. Congratulations on your recent publications! Keep writing more."

"Thanks for the little pearls of wisdom and optimism."

Introduction

To the reader:

As I write this book I'm facing some difficult challenges in my life. I'm writing many of these quotes to inspire and encourage myself. I don't know your situation, but I hope that these words of wisdom, encouragement, and inspiration can help you in your situation. If you're already satisfied and content with life, this book will inspire you to keep living a full happy life.

For frequent words of encouragement, [click here to follow me on Twitter @calvinklee2010](). I often post inspirational quotes. I've tweeted over 1,000 times and I'm sure you'll be encouraged and inspired by my Twitter. Some of the words of wisdom in this book are taken from my tweets over the past few years.

Besides being an author, I also enjoy composing music. I once wrote a very happy and bright song that when people heard it, they thought I wrote the song when I was very happy. The opposite is true: I wrote the happy song in some of my saddest moments. I wrote the happy song to encourage myself, and know in time I will leave my sadness behind and experience happiness once again.

In difficult moments, you and I both know it's a challenge to stay positive and hopeful. Yet it is precisely these moments that you and I must speak positive words of wisdom, encouragement, and inspiration. Speak them to yourself and to the people around you, and watch your days become better and then come brighter days. If you want to live an extraordinary life, I recommend you read my book _"Living an Extraordinary and Amazingly Purposeful Life."_

I hope you will find wisdom, encouragement, and inspiration.

Calvin K. Lee

November 2015

1. How to be successful

Thomas Edison took more than 1,000 attempts to invent the electric light bulb. Did he say he failed 1,000 times? No, he said he was successful in finding 1,000 ways *not* to make a light bulb.

With every rejection, you are one step closer to success.

You reap what you sow. What you don't sow is what you won't reap.

There is a fire of passion inside of you. All you have to do is find it and rekindle it.

All successful people have a clear purpose and goal.

Thinking is hard work, which is why so few people do it. Those who can think succeed.

Everyone has the potential to succeed. Frequently it's not a lack of skill that prevents people from success, but rather fear: fear of the unknown, fear of rejection, fear of success, fear of rejection, fear of being different. What do you fear?

It is said the journey of a thousand miles begins with a single step. Success does not come overnight, it comes through a series of steps. Sometimes it's two steps forward and one step back.

Don't despair. Every setback and rejection brings you one step closer to your goal.

You know you can do it. Believe in yourself!

If it is to be, why not me?

Successful people are always looking for opportunities to help others. Unsuccessful people are always asking, "What's in it for me?"

If you've never failed, it means you've never tried. If you've never tried things beyond your comfort zone, you've likely never failed.

Money spent can be re-earned, but experience is mine to keep for the rest of my life.

If you want to succeed, cut the following from your vocabulary: "I should have", "I could have", "I would have". Now take concrete action.

The difference between winners and ordinary people is winners follow through despite fear while others just dream and take no action.

Learning to delay instant gratification is crucial to success. A research study put a child in an empty room with a cookie in front of them. The researcher tells the child he will leave the room for a while. The child can choose to take the cookie, but if the child can wait until the researcher comes back, the researcher will give the child two cookies. The research showed children that can wait and delay instant gratification are more successful in life.

2. Be thankful

Be thankful today that you're alive and breathing and have a life. Some people after a severe injury to the brain and body are in a persistent vegetative state.

Be thankful you can walk. Many disabled people don't have that privilege.

Be thankful that you have two functional arms. Some people can't use their arms and they need people to help them get dressed and use the toilet.

Be thankful that you can eat and swallow. Some people can't enjoy food and drinks because they are fed intravenously in their arm.

Be thankful you have enough to eat. Many people in Third World countries barely have enough to eat.

Be thankful for clean water you can drink and bathe. Many people in other parts of the world don't have safe drinking water.

Be thankful for education. Many people in other parts of the world are illiterate and have no hope of getting out of poverty.

Be thankful for your friends and family. Some people are in loneliness and are aching for love.

Be thankful for your pains and bad situations. Pick yourself up and go comfort others in similar situations. The best people to comfort those who are hurting are those who have been through similar situations. People who have survived cancer best comfort cancer patients.

Be thankful you can have dreams and goals. They make life worth living.

3. Words of encouragement in pain and suffering

Problems teach us life lessons that smooth sailing days don't. When you're waiting, you are learning patience.

Don't say, "Impossible", think, "I'm possible".

A person's pain tolerance can increase. Athletes have trained themselves to endure great pain in order to reach a goal. You have heard the saying "no pain, no gain."

If you feel pain and suffering, know that someone else in the world is in much more pain and suffering than you.

Not satisfied with your life? Someone would gladly trade his or her life for yours.

The more successful you are, the more responsibility you have.

Life is about problem solving. You've solved numerous problems in the past and can do it again.

Life is a roller coaster. Sometimes you hit the lows and sometimes you hit the highs.

You might not be able to change your circumstances, but you can change your attitude towards the situation. Change what you can, not what you cannot.

Smile despite being in pain. You will feel better.

Make the most out of a bad situation.

In your pain and suffering, go and help others. You will cheer yourself up and also give hope to those suffering around you.

Believe that good things will happen to you. We are self-fulfilling prophecies. If we always think we'll be in pain and suffering, that's what you will get in life. If you believe your life will change for the better, it will come to you.

Too many people wait for things to happen for them in life instead of proactively making them happen. Take baby steps, do whatever you can.

Hope that is seen is no hope at all. Who hopes for what he or she already has? But if we hope for what we do not have, we wait for it patiently.

4. A brighter day will surely come
Need encouragement for a brighter day? Click here to listen to the song "A Brighter Day", which I listen to every time I need encouragement for a brighter day.

Rainy days may be gloomy, but remember its positive sides: rain nourishes the soil of crops that is our food. Without rain humans can't survive.

In tough times we usually focus on our problems and magnify them bigger than they really are. But problems are sometimes a blessing in disguise.

Rainy days may be gloomy, but they make us appreciate the sunny days more.

Losing what you have makes you learn to appreciate what you have when you have it.

If we look hard enough in hindsight, rainy days serve a purpose in our lives.

We grow more in challenging times than we do in smooth sailing days.

High school is harder than elementary school. University is harder than high school. Each step along the way you find challenges, but trust you'll grow and conquer whatever challenges life throws your way, like you always have done in the past.

In rainy days, do two things: (1) be thankful and find things to be grateful about, (2) remember your past successes and breakthroughs.

Nobody is free from trouble. Not even the people that appears successful and happy all the time. If you knew what they're really going through in life, you might not envy them.

The troubles you are facing are common to mankind. Nothing is new, just variations on the same theme. Someone has encountered the same problems as you and has overcome them.

Trouble times teaches us patience. Patience is one of the hardest life lessons to learn, but necessary if we want to succeed.

Bookkeeping & Accounting Explained

If you've failed and tried your best, pat yourself in the back. Get up stronger and try again with your new experience. You will succeed!

5. Words of wisdom on love

Love is to accept a person with their blemishes, imperfections, warts, and failures.

You are more blessed to give love than to receive love.

The more love you give, the more love you will receive.

Love is a very strong bond known to human kind.

Focus on the other person rather than yourself.

In order to connect with other people, you need to take off your mask and be vulnerable. Weaknesses bond people together.

Men, women are not to be understood. Women are to be accepted.

Women, men are not to be understood. Men are to be accepted.

Be comfortable with being different. Communicate your needs to your loved ones.

If you have not learned to love, you have not learned to live.

Love is powerful and mysterious. You can never learn all the ways to love. It will take you a lifetime.

The more love you feel, the happier you will be.

You are loved dearly by someone.

Love is not only a fleeting feeling, but also a commitment. This is true love.

Love people for who they really are, just as you want people to love you for whom you really are.

Love is a verb. Love requires action.

Everybody needs love. It is an essential thing. We *crave* love.

Love those who don't deserve your love. You will benefit from the experience whether others accept you or not.

6. You are unique!

Only you have the unique combination - background, education, experience, quirks, skills, strengths & weaknesses – to be you. Nobody thinks exactly like you or act exactly like you in all situations. This is good. If you look hard enough, you will find there are some things only you can do that others can't.

Accept and embrace yourself, including strengths & weaknesses, warts, faults, past history, mistakes. Only then can you move forward.

Unsatisfied with the way something is done? Do something about it! Create something new and recruit people to your cause.

The hardest thing for me to learn is to unlearn old ways of thinking.

The most common regret of dying people: not living a life true to themselves, and living a life others expect them to live.

What do you do well? What can you do, but not well? What can you do, but dislike doing?

To build up others, you must first build up yourself. There comes a time, however, when the former becomes more important than the latter.

Be yourself, no matter how difficult it is to be.

There is someone out there who will love you exactly for who you are.

There will only be one you throughout history of mankind. There will be none before you and none after you with exactly the same traits, skills, and experiences as you. You are unique!

7. Fake it till you make it!
Fake it till you make it.

Always keep improving yourself. Once you stop learning and improving yourself, others will get ahead of you.

Learning is a great joy in itself.

We only use 10% of our brains. Think about the potential possibilities!

How we think affects how we act. But how we act also affects how we feel. Try this: hold your head up high, bring your shoulders back, walk as straight and confidently looking as you can. You will start to feel more confident.

Everyone can learn public speaking. First deal with your fear, then practice, practice, practice.

You are learning since the day you were born.

You are a better version of yourself today than you were yesterday.

Always strive for excellence. Do everything you can with what you have.

Think and imagine the possibilities!

Believe in yourself. You can do it!

Everybody starts learning a new skill from zero experience. You learned to ride a bicycle with zero experience. You learned a new subject in school with zero experience. You are amazing. You can learn new skills and gain new experiences.

8. More words of wisdom

Having one more friend is better than having one more enemy.

Don't burn any bridges. This is a very small world. People know people and they talk.

Listen to classical music. Music gives inspiration and creativity. Studies show children that listen to Mozart have better memories and cognitive learning abilities.

Do everything in moderation. Too much of a good thing may be harmful.

Buying books are a wise investment. You learn valuable life lessons from experienced people and you don't have to make the same mistakes from them.

Don't be afraid to be an innovator or inventor. You may be mocked and ridiculed for your novice ideas, but you know you're right.

Experts aren't always right. Galileo thought the earth revolved around the sun. "Experts" in Galileo's time

Bookkeeping & Accounting Explained

thought the universe revolved around the earth. "Experts" once thought the earth was flat. They thought Columbus would sail to the edge of the earth and fall off.

When you help others they will usually reciprocate when you need help.

If you enjoyed this book, please support me by leaving a positive review on Amazon. Click here to review. Alternatively, scroll to the end of this book and click on the stars and leave a review. As a bonus, after you leave a review, e-mail me at hellocalvinlee@gmail.com and I'll send you a FREE PDF version of this book. When I see a review, I am more encouraged to write more books.

Join my Facebook author fan page for new books:
https://www.facebook.com/hellocalvinlee/

Final Thoughts

We accumulate wisdom through life experiences. As we go through life, we can choose to see the glass as half full or half empty. Each of us chooses (consciously or unconsciously) how we think. If we think we can, we will take positive constructive actions. If we think we can't, we shut down our brains and we give up before we even try.

How a person thinks greatly affects his or her life. It's like placing a filter in which the eyes look through. If you put in a gray filter, you will see everything as gray in life. If you put in a brightly colorful filter, you will see brightly colorful things in life.

No one is free from worries, troubles, problems, and difficulties. Everyone faces them at many times in life. Even though some people seem to have life all together, sometimes it's an act. We can all use words of wisdom, encouragement, and inspiration at times.

I encourage you to share words of wisdom, encouragement, and inspiration to your family and friends. First, it brightens up your day. Then you can share it and brighten up the day of people around you. Be a blessing to others besides just saying "Bless you!" when they sneeze.

I have always dreamed of writing and publishing my own books. This dream has become a reality. This is my third book, and I was very excited to see my previous two books being downloaded over 130 times in 3 days in North America, Europe, Asia, and South America. This is quite an exciting journey for me. If you enjoy my books, please rate them on Amazon and leave a comment. This will let other people see readers like you enjoyed the book and so more people can benefit from it.

BONUS book #4:

"How to Work Smarter, Not Harder: Success in the Workplace"

©2015 Calvin Lee
All rights reserved

This book or any portion thereof may not be reproduced or used
without written permission of the author/publisher
except in brief quotations, book reviews, and articles.

HOW TO WORK SMARTER, NOT HARDER (BOOK #4)

CALVIN K. LEE, MBA, CPA

Success in the Workplace

Table of Contents

Introduction: smart ways to work

1. Techniques to instantly brighten up your day: smile and whistle

2. Working smarter: know if you're a morning person or a night owl

3. Change your attitude and approach

4. Exercise becomes more important as busyness increases

5. Improve your biggest asset: your mind

6. Meditation: it gives you a sense of more time

7. Improve your creativity by doing something relaxing

8. Know yourself: your personality, likes & dislikes, strengths & weaknesses

9. Avoid multitasking: finish one task before starting another

10. Improve attention span

Final Thoughts

Introduction: smart ways to work

There are many ways to work, but some ways are smarter than other ways. For example, how many ways there are to get from San Francisco to New York City? Here are some options:

1. Walk there
2. Run there
3. Ride a bicycle there
4. Drive a car there
5. Take a plane there

All of these ways will get you from San Francisco to New York City…eventually. It's just that some ways are smarter than other ways. All of these ways eventually work, but some ways are smarter and more efficient than others. In today's day and age, time is of the essence. You've heard the saying, "Time is money."

KEY POINT: there are multiple ways to solve every problem, but some ways are smarter than other ways.

Some of the suggestions in this book can be implemented immediately and effortlessly, immediately improving your work life. Other suggestions take time to change an old habit to a new one. Be patient with yourself while trying to change. It takes effort but you will receive huge dividends later.

Kids are incredibly creative. If you ask them to stand in the corner and face the wall, they will find a fun way to spend the time there. They will invent a game with himself or herself, sing a song, wave their arms, or see how long they can hold their breath.

I love watching kids play at the park. They are incredibly creative in what they do. They don't need people to tell them how to play. They innately know how to have fun. Unfortunately, as we grow to be adults we lose that sense of creativity. We think there is one "right" way to do things, and we do it over and over again. Fortunately for us, we all have a kid living inside of us. We were once kids, with limitless imagination and energy. But our school system taught us to sit still, learn the 'right' way to do things, and just follow what others do.

KEY POINT: Each of us can let the creative child inside of us be imaginative and have fun. In the creative process, you'll find smarter ways to work!

We can tap into our imagination and find smarter ways to do things. Let the creative child inside of you blossom again. You'll experience life in a whole new way doing your routine tasks!

PUT IT INTO ACTION: For every task you do, try to find a smarter way to do it. Be creative and have some fun!

1. Techniques to instantly brighten up your day: smile and whistle

If you're in a happy mood, you work smarter than when you are in a grumpy mood. There are many simple ways to lift your mood and brighten up your day within minutes.

KEY POINT: You work smarter when you're in a good mood.

The first way is to smile, whether you feel like it or not. Once I was really stressed out at work. I had nothing to smile about, but I forced my face to smile. Doing that changes the chemistry in your body that actually makes you feel better. It's true when you feel a certain emotion, your body would physically mimic that emotion. For example, if you feel happy, your face would naturally smile. The reverse is also true. If you make your body physically do something, you will start feeling the accompanying emotion.

Another way to instantly brighten up your day is to whistle, or hum a song. It's hard to whistle and feel grumpy at the same time. You've probably heard the song lyrics that go, "whistle while you work." It will make you happier instantly. Then you can work smarter.

PUT IT INTO ACTION: smile even if you don't feel like it. Whistle if your work place allows it, or hum quietly to yourself. All of these simple yet powerful techniques can lift your mood within a short period of time and significantly improve the quality of your work. You can also try other actions like snapping your fingers or clapping your hands.

2. Working smarter: know if you're a morning person or a night owl

I'm a morning person. I'm mentally most alert and creative in the mornings. That's why I do my most important work in the mornings, work that requires brainpower and creativity. I leave my routine work for the afternoon or evening. When I read, I find I focus the best in the morning. I do my planning and big tasks in the morning.

Other people are night owls. They work best late a night. They do their best work at night. If you're a night owl, you may want to adjust your tasks so that you set your schedule and function at your best.

KEY POINT: Some people are morning persons and some people are night owls.

Each person is different, so you really have to experiment what works best for you. Pay attention to the time of the day when you feel freshest, and use that valuable time to do your most important work. Leave the lesser important tasks to other parts of the day after your most important work is done.

This also means you need to prioritize your work. If done correctly, it takes little time to plan and prioritize, but saves huge amounts of time when executing the tasks throughout your day. On the other hand, if you don't prioritize your work, you may end up doing lesser tasks first that you enjoy more, and leave the more important tasks till last minute then you're scrambling to catch up and hand in poor quality work that can hurt you on your next performance review with your manager.

PUT IT INTO ACTION: Find out if you're a morning person or a night owl. After that, prioritize your most important work to the time when you are mentally freshest.

3. Change your attitude and approach

If you want to work smarter, you need to change your attitude and approach.

One definition of insanity is to keep doing the same thing and expect different results. So many people try to reach a goal but fail because they don't change their methods. Some people try to lose weight, but fail time and again with weight loss programs. Some people try to become rich, but keep doing the same things and habits that keep them poor. We fail because we fail to change our attitude and approach.

KEY POINT: you need to change your attitude and approach in order to improve.

So how can we succeed? We need to study successful people. See how they think and act. Find successful people and ask them to show you how they became successful.

It's difficult to break old habits and form new ones. It can take a few weeks or more to change a habit. It takes conscious effort. Every learning curve has four quadrants, moving in a clockwise direction from *un*consciously *in*competent to consciously *in*competent to consciously **competent** to *un*consciously **competent**. Visualize it.

1. Unconsciously incompetent	2. Consciously incompetent
4. Unconsciously competent	3. Consciously competent

Starting in the top left quadrant, unconsciously incompetent means you didn't know you were incompetent at something. Let's say you want to learn to drive. You start in the first quadrant, unconsciously incompetent, meaning you didn't know you were incompetent. Once you decided to learn to drive, you now are in the second quadrant, consciously aware you are incompetent. You struggle with learn how to drive. You make mistakes.

Moving onto the third quadrant, you have now had some success learning to drive, but it takes conscious effort. With more practice, you move onto the fourth quadrant, where you don't even have to consciously think about your driving. You just do it on autopilot.

In order to work smarter, you have to go through the four quadrants. It takes time and effort to change habits and form new habits, but it is well worth the effort in increased efficiency and more productivity.

PUT IT INTO ACTION: consciously choose a task you want to learn. Practice until you can subconsciously do the task competently.

4. Exercise becomes more important as busyness increases

As I was doing my master's degree, the end of term was drawing near. This means many exams, term papers, and projects are becoming due. Many of my classmates got into the trenches and spent hours studying, writing papers or doing projects. Usually the first thing to go is exercise. When people become busy, they can easily say, "I'm too busy to go to the gym."

I do the opposite. The more busy and stressful my schedule, the more important exercise becomes. Experts have explained the many benefits of exercise, including reducing stress, improving attention span, makes a person feel happier through release of endorphins, better blood circulation which means better concentration, and overall makes a person work more efficiently.

KEY POINT: exercise improves your focus and concentration, reduces stress, and improves the quality of your work.

I find that by doing exercise, I work more efficiently. I feel better about myself. In fact, doing exercise actually *saves me more* time instead of take up time. I think one reason why people have to work long hours is because they are not functioning at their maximum efficiency, and part of the reason is they don't exercise their bodies.

I truly believe if I take care of my body, my body will take care of me. If I take care of my body, it will operate at maximum efficiency. I can work faster, make fewer mistakes, get sick less often. The excuse "I don't have time" usually just means whatever you say you don't have time for is low priority. I prioritize exercise and will make time for it.

If your mother gets seriously ill and taken to the hospital, you'd drop everything and rush to see her right away. This is because you prioritize your mother over your usual work. If you say, "I don't have time to visit my mother who is seriously ill in the hospital, I need to finish this proposal", you are implying she is a low priority in your life and your work has higher priority. If you lose your job you can always find another one, but you will only have one mother. You choose your priorities. Whatever takes priority you will always find time.

PUT IT INTO ACTION: prioritize exercise and schedule time to exercise. Your body will thank you, and you'll find smarter ways to work.

5. Improve your biggest asset: your mind

The mind is like a muscle. The more you use it, the stronger and healthier it gets. Memory works like a muscle. The more you use it, the better it becomes.

With the invention of smart phones, the need to memorize things has been replaced with the convenience of technology. It is so easy to become lazy and stop using our brains when we so over rely on technology. People used to remember their friends' telephone numbers. I don't think as many people can remember their friends' telephone numbers now that they can just tap a few buttons on their smart phone's memory to dial a number.

KEY POINT: your mind is your greatest asset. Take care of it.

Many people stop putting effort into learning as soon as they graduate from university. In order to work smarter, you need to make sure that your mind stays sharp. My boss worked well past the usual retirement age. His body aged, but his mind was still sharp. He kept using his brain at work, and continually seeks new challenges, reading books, and doing charity work.

The best way to keep the mind healthy is to continually learn new things and seek challenges. Try learning a new language. Studies have shown evidence that people that know multiple languages have a lower chance of Alzheimer's disease than people that only know one language. Try learning a new sport or musical instrument. Music trains the right brain, which improves creativity.

PUT IT INTO ACTION: exercise your brain and use it often. Find new challenges and learn new things to keep your brain in shape.

6. Meditation: it gives you a sense of more time

With today's fast-paced, hustle & bustle world, taking time out to quiet the mind is becoming scarcer. What I've found is that meditation helps to calm and quiet the brain by focusing on my breathing. I'm a person who likes action so it's difficult to sit quietly and concentrate on my breath. But I've found that when I'm tired and easily irritable, if I just take 5 or 10 minutes to sit quietly and concentrate on my breath, my concentration and attention returns to me. I feel my concentration is restored, less tired, more focused, and more energetic.

As I'm writing this book, it's late into the night. I've had several meetings today and it's been an exhausting day. I decided to take 20 minutes to meditate and concentrate on my breath, and after 20 minutes, I feel more energetic and actually can write my book. If I didn't meditate, I would feel tired and not have any ideas flow to write on.

The Bible tells Christians to meditate on the Word of God day and night. Meditation is about focusing on something, and blocking out distractions. It calms a wandering mind. Wandering minds usually lead to worry, fear, and confusion.

KEY POINT: Meditation calms and quiets your mind, revitalizes energy, and lets you work smarter.

If you do a Google search, you can find many websites on how to meditate. The great thing about meditation is that it can be done almost anywhere, anytime. Here are some ways to start meditating:

1. Sit quietly with your back straight.
2. Close your eyes if it helps you concentrate.
3. Relax every muscle in your body.
4. Breathe deeply through your nose, letting your belly expand. If your belly doesn't expand and only your chest expands, you need to relax more. Most people only expand their chest when they breathe, and this causes shallow breathing.
5. Concentrate on your breath. If your mind wanders, gently acknowledge the thought, and let it go, and return to concentrating on your breath.

Start with a few minutes, and work your way up to 20 minutes or more. Meditation calms the mind, reduces stress, revitalizes energy, and makes you feel like you've got more time. If you find your mind wandering, be gentle with yourself. Just gently acknowledge whatever thoughts you have, then guide your focus back to your breath.

With your mind and body revitalized, you can now work smarter!

PUT IT INTO ACTION: start meditating today for a few minutes. If you don't have the time, just take 3 deep breaths and focus on your breathing.

7. Improve your creativity by doing something relaxing

Inventors, authors, and musicians have reported that their inspiration comes to them at the least expected times. Sometimes ideas just don't flow when you're sitting at your desk. Creative ideas come when you're taking a walk, taking a bath, or just doing something relaxing.

The mind works in amazing ways. Creativity usually flows when the mind is relaxed. So if you're trying to come up with some creative ideas, try going for a walk or something that relaxes you.

Some musician composers get their creativity while at a restaurant, and jot down their music right there on the restaurant napkins! Do a Google search for more details.

KEY POINT: creative ideas come when your mind is relaxed.

Do you need to do something creative? Your creative ideas might just come to you when you least expect it. The ideas may not come while you're sitting at your desk. The subconscious mind is a really fascinating subject to study. Different visual cues cause different chemical reactions in the brain. A change of scenery such as going on vacation can relax a person and let them feel refreshed.

Perhaps that great idea you've been waiting for will come to you during or shortly after you take a vacation!

During stressful times, our minds can shut down. Creative processes are not available. Taking a weekend retreat, going camping, taking a nature hike, or going swimming in a beautiful lake may just be the cure.

After you take time to enjoy and relax, you'll find smarter ways to work.

PUT IT INTO ACTION: take frequent breaks. Take a walk. Listen to some relaxing music. Go on vacation. It will let you work smarter.

8. Know yourself: your personality, likes & dislikes, strengths & weaknesses

It's amazing how little we know about ourselves. We think we know ourselves, but there are a lot of things we don't know about ourselves. Other people can see things that we don't see about ourselves.

You may think you're suitable for one career, but a career consultant may see other traits in you that may help you work smarter and have a more fulfilling career. For example, I've been an accountant for most of my career. When I met with a career consultant and did a paid career assessment test, he asked me have I considered several other career options! Some of the options I've thought about, some of the others I've never considered!

KEY POINT: feedback from other people can allow you to learn about yourself.

Some people choose their careers based on stability or pay, but absolutely hate their job. It's sad that they spend most of the prime years of their lives doing something they don't enjoy. That's why doing personality tests like the *Myers-Briggs personality indicator* with the four letter code (i.e. ENTP or ISFJ) that determines your personality as extroverted or introverted, sensing or intuitive, thinking or judging, and perceiving or judging may help you understand why you prefer to do things certain ways different from other people with different personalities.

The *Birkman Method Assessment* for work preferences may also be good idea. I recently took the *Birkman Method Assessment* with a one-hour consulting session with certified Birkman consultant Jonathan Michael and it revealed things about myself at work that I did not even realize. I was surprised and learned something about myself. These assessments may cost a little money, but can spare you a lot of pain of being in the wrong job, which is much more costly emotionally and financially in the long run.

Once you find the right job for your personality and strengths, you can work smarter and be a lot happier!

PUT IT INTO ACTION: find out everything you can about yourself. Do reflection, pay attention to how you think, and ask other people for feedback.

9. Avoid multitasking: finish one task before starting another

When the word "multitasking" was invented, almost every single job posting asked for candidates who can multitask. Studies have now shown that humans aren't really capable of multitasking. What happens when we think we're multitasking is that we quickly shift our attention from one task to another task.

KEYPOINT: multitasking means breaking focus from one task to switch to another task.

The problem with this is that it takes time and effort to adjust to a different task, and efficiency actually decreases. It is better to focus and finish a task before moving onto a second task. One reason that contributes to so many people being stressed and burning out is because they are continually distracted by people, tasks, and technology that beeps and buzzes at them.

I watched a video recently where some people did an interesting experiment. They hung over 100 one-dollar bills on a tree on a busy street. They wanted to see how many people would see and take the free money. Interestingly, many people who walked by the tree were too distracted to notice. They were either looking at their smart phones or thinking about thoughts in their minds while they walk. They walked right past the tree with over 100 one-dollar bills hanging on the leaves without even noticing the free money. You can do a Google search to find the video.

When we walk, our mind can easily go on autopilot, especially if we walk on a familiar street. We don't notice things. This may be good, because if we have to consciously respond to every stimuli, our mind will be overwhelmed. Our mind subconsciously tunes out some stimuli so that we are not overwhelmed. But if our mind is always on autopilot, we miss the here and now, and are not living in the present. We miss out on living our lives.

Sometimes when I walk I focus on the bottom of my feet as they touch the ground. This helps my mind stay in the present. To live life fully means to live in the present. To work smarter means to put your mind to what you are doing.

PUT IT INTO ACTION: finish one task before starting a new one. You'll be more efficient and feel less stressful.

10. Improve attention span

Studies have shown that people who give presentations in the past had more than a few minutes to capture the attention of their audience. Nowadays, if a presenter doesn't capture the attention of their audience within minutes, someone's going to whip out their smart phone and start checking messages.

KEY POINT: technology is great, but it diminishes our attention span.

Smart phones and other electronic devices have contributed to shorter attention spans. A study of toddlers that are given a smart phone or a tablet to play with show that they get irritable and throw tantrums when they don't get to play with those devices. The same goes with adults. The continuous beeping and buzzing of smart devices when messages and e-mails are received creates an addictive behaviour to checking our phones.

Control the use of your smart devices; don't let your smart devices control you. I turn off many of the default notifications on my smart phone.

To improve your attention span, try meditation. Try setting aside your phone during dinnertime. Try to be fully present at each and every moment.

With an improved attention span, you will find ways to work smarter.

PUT IT INTO ACTION: set some limits on your usage of smart devices. Be respectful during face to face meetings, meals, and gatherings, and put away your smart devices, and resist the urge to keep checking your messages.

Final thoughts

I enjoyed sharing the suggestions in this book with you on working smarter from my own life. I sincerely hope you've enjoyed this book and found some good suggestions to apply to your own life. I suggest you start with one or two and implement it into your routine. Remember it takes a few weeks for a new habit to form, and it takes conscious effort at first. But once you've formed the habit it will become effortless when you are unconsciously competent.

Bookkeeping & Accounting Explained

BONUS book #5:

"A Collection of Short Stories"
©2015 Calvin Lee
All rights reserved

This book or any portion thereof may not be reproduced or used without written permission of the author/publisher except in brief quotations, book reviews, and articles.

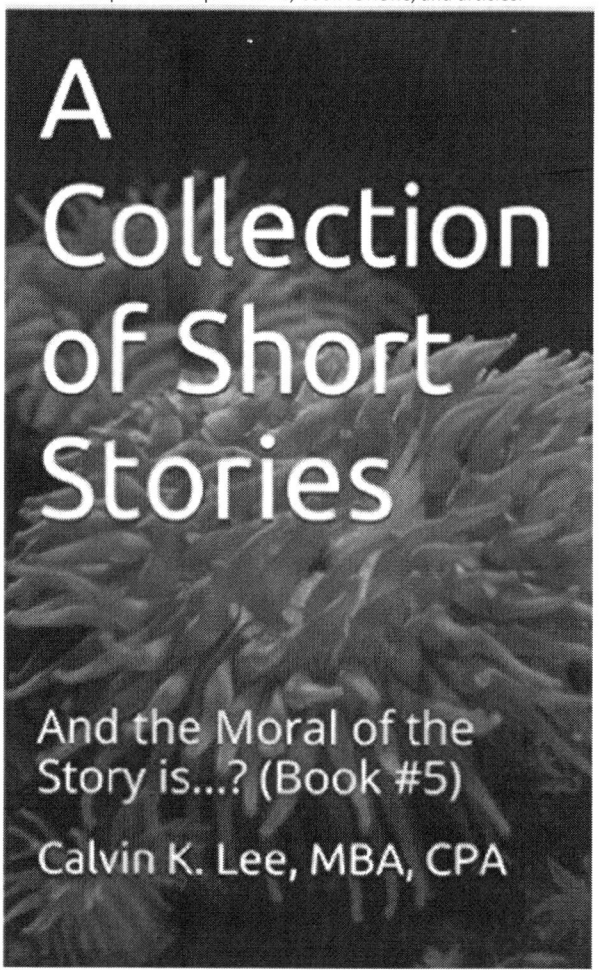

A Collection of Short Stories

And the Moral of the Story is...? (Book #5)

Calvin K. Lee, MBA, CPA

Table of Contents

To the reader

The flag and pole (adapted from the blockbuster movie Captain America)

The red and blue crayons

The train

Five planks of wood: unity is power

The magical watches

A school of fish

The well

The animal trap and a benevolent man

Contact the author and final words

Other books by Calvin K. Lee

To the reader

Stories have been used throughout history to pass knowledge and history from generation to generation. They can also be used to teach a lesson or demonstrate a point. In this book of short stories, I want to ignite your imagination and think about the moral of the stories. My boss, who is a master storyteller, loved to come out of his office and ask his staff, "And the moral of the story is…?" and my colleagues and I would say, "Eat more spaghetti!" Sometimes my colleague Jonathan would say for fun, "Ford is better than GM!" because he drives a Ford and the boss drives a GM. We'd all get a good laugh. I love my boss and colleagues.

Some of the stories are my own original stories. One is adapted from a movie scene from the blockbuster movie Captain America. Some are adapted from morals of folk stories that I've updated with a modern twist.

This is my 5th book. I have been incredibly blessed to be able to write and publish my previous 4 books in a span of two weeks. The ideas and my creativity flowed like water to me. As I was having dinner with a friend of mine, she asked me if I ever thought about writing stories. I actually really enjoyed writing detective stories when I was in grade 2. We had a Creative Writing class, and I always looked forward to writing my detective stories. I wrote lots of stories. Unfortunately, the early manuscripts from my elementary school days are lost.

For over 10 years I have written blog articles about life, health, school, career, and other topics on Xanga, Wordpress, and Facebook. Many of my friends have provided positive feedback, so I decided to expand my horizons and share my writings with the world. Thanks to Amazon, my dream of writing books, publishing them, and letting people around the globe benefit has become a reality. I published my first book on November 1, 2015, and in the two weeks that have gone by I have been shocked and overwhelmed, where approximately 300 copies of my books have been downloaded in Australia, Brazil, Canada, France, Germany, India, Japan, Spain, U.K., and U.S. I feel incredibly blessed and thankful for everyone's support.

The flag and pole (adapted from the blockbuster movie *Captain America*)

You can find a video clip of this on Youtube by searching "Captain America pole scene".

A drill sergeant told his unit of soldiers that they were going to have a test. The test will test their physical strength and decision-making ability.

First, the sergeant made the soldiers do pushups. Then they had to crawl through mud. After that they had to run miles throughout the training fields.

Finally, they arrived at their final test. The drill sergeant stood next to tall pole and shouted, "Listen up, soldiers! There's a flag attached to the top of this pole. The first person to get it and bring me the flag passes the test. The rest will have to do pushups, crawl through the mud, and run miles again."

The men jumped on the pole one by one and tried to climb up the pole to get the flag. However, the sergeant in advance had coated the pole with oil so it was really slippery and the soldiers couldn't get a solid grip to climb. They kept sliding back down, often landing on top of each other. "Nobody's gotten that flag in 17 years!" shouted the drill sergeant. After many failed attempts, the soldiers were exhausted and was considering giving up, that the task was impossible.

At this time one of the soldiers, Rogers, walked up to the pole and said he will get the flag. The other soldiers, who were bigger and stronger than Rogers, laughed. They called him "Skinny Rogers" because of his lack of physical strength and skinny frame.

Rogers walked up to the pole, and calmly pulled out the metal piece out of the ground that held the pole vertical. The pole fell to the ground with a thud like a tree being cut down, leaving the flag that was on top of the pole on the ground.

"Hey, that's cheating!" said the other soldiers.

Rogers calmly said, "The sergeant just told to get the flag and bring it to him. He never said taking the pole down was against the rules." Rogers then looked at the sergeant.

"He is correct!" said the sergeant with a smile. "This is not only a test of physical strength, but a test of your decision-making skills and ability to carefully pay attention to instructions! Now all of you, with the exception of Rogers, do your pushups, crawl through the mud, and run miles again!"

The red and blue crayons

Jill and Jane were friends in a grade 1 classroom. They did everything together: ate their lunches together, walked home from school together, and did homework together. One day, they went to art class. The teacher gave Jill and Jane a large piece of paper each. She gave Jill a red crayon and gave Jane a blue crayon.

"Ok, Jill and Jane. I want the two of you to draw me a bunch of purple grapes," said the teacher.

Jill and Jane stared at each other. Then they turned their attention to their pieces of paper and started drawing. Jill drew a bunch of red grapes, and Jane drew a bunch of blue grapes. They handed their papers to the teacher, who shook her head and said, "I want a bunch of *purple* grapes. Not red or blue grapes."

Jill and Jane stared at each other again. "Let's switch crayons and try again," Jill said to Jane. Jane thought it was a good idea so they switched their crayons. This time, Jill drew a bunch of blue grapes, and Jane drew red grapes. It's still not what the teacher wanted.

Jane said to Jill, "Give me your piece of paper." Jill gave her blue grapes drawing to Jane. Jane then used her red crayon to draw over Jill's blue grapes. The blue color and red color blended together to result in purple grapes.

"What an excellent idea!" said Jill, "Now you give me your red grapes."

Jane handed her drawing of red grapes to Jane, who used her blue crayon to color the red grapes, which blended into purple grapes.

The teacher was pleased how they combined their colors to create a new color. Individually, Jill and Jane's red and blue crayons can only produce red and blue grapes. By combining their crayon colors, they produced the desired purple grapes.

The train

A man was walking along a train track. Suddenly he heard the sound of a train coming towards him in the distant. He ran towards the train for 100 meters before jumping off the track.

Why?

He was in a tunnel.

Sometimes life is like that. We have to run courageously towards our problems.

Five planks of wood: unity is power

A man has five sons. He owns a family business inherited from his own father, and his five sons work at his company. He wants his five sons to take over when he retires, but he was worried because they did not get along with each other.

In an effort to unite his sons, the father gathered them on a basketball court. His sons were all trained in karate and self-defense since they were young. He took out a stack of rectangular planks of wood.

He called his eldest son over to himself, gave him a plank of wood, and said, "Break this piece of wood with a karate chop."

"No problem," said his eldest son with a smirk. With one swift karate chop, the wood easily snapped in two.

"Good, you've practiced your karate," said the father. "Here are two pieces of wood. Stack them on top of each other and break them with one karate chop."

"That's still not too hard," said his eldest son. With one swing of his hand he broke the two pieces of wood.

The father then gave him three pieces of wood. The eldest son was able to break them, but with considerable effort. Then the father gave him four pieces of wood. The eldest son had to use all his might to break them.

Finally, the father gave him five pieces of wood. Not wanting to be embarrassed in front of his siblings, the eldest son tried again and again, and couldn't break the five pieces of wood stacked on each other. His hand hurt so much after a few attempts. Finally he gave up and told his father it's impossible.

The father motioned his second eldest son to come over to try to break the five pieces of wood. The second eldest son couldn't do it either.

The third, fourth, and youngest sons also tried to break the five pieces of wood. They too, failed.

The father said to them, "If the five of you unite and work to build this family business together, you will be like these five planks of wood. You will be prosperous and no one can beat you. But if you don't work together, your competitors will break you and overwhelm you."

The magical watches

Once upon a time there was a man and a woman who were very afraid of public speaking. Every time they stood in front of people they would just freeze and forget what they were going to say. But they were both in the same company training to become professional public speakers.

One day, the two of them were sitting inside a restaurant enjoying coffees after a meal. They noticed there was a strange looking lamp on the table, and decided to take a closer look. They rubbed the lamp, and out popped a genie. The two of them were shocked, but none of the other people in the restaurant seem to be able to see or hear the genie.

"I am the answer to your wishes," said the genie. "Instead of three wishes I will grant your wish of being able to do public speaking well." The men and woman were delighted.

"I will give you each two choices, and you can choose only one. The first choice is a watch that when you wear it, you will be able to do public speaking perfectly immediately."

"The second choice is a watch that when you wear it, you won't get good at public speaking right away. Every time you wear the watch, you get a little better. When you get to your 100th speech, your public speaking will be perfect."

The man and the woman stared at each other, amazed at their good fortune.

The man said to the genie: "I'll take the watch that allows me to do public speaking perfectly immediately."

The woman said to the genie: "I'll take the watch that doesn't make me a perfect public speaker right away, but will allow me to get better each time I do public speaking, and by my 100th speech, my public speaking will be perfect."

"Your wish is my command," said the genie. Two watches appeared out of nowhere. Then the genie and the lamp disappeared. The man and the woman took their watches and happily left the restaurant.

The man that got the watch that instantly makes him do public speaking perfectly suddenly became the star public speaker of his company. It took him no effort to speak well, and he won numerous awards and speaking contracts. On the other hand, the woman struggled with public speaking at first, but after 100 public speaking engagements, she perfected the art of public speaking.

One day, the CEO of their company told the man and the woman: "You two are our company's best public speakers. I want you each to train a new class of amateurs into professional public speakers."

The man became scared. With the watch the genie gave him, he never struggled with public speaking. Whenever he put on the watch, he just spoke perfectly. He couldn't relate to the struggles his class of students experienced in public speaking. His class performed poorly.

The woman who took 100 public speaking engagements to perfect public speaking was able to share with her class the struggles as she learned to speak. She was able to relate to the struggles of her students, and was able to help them improve. Her class performed well.

Some time later, the CEO of their company told the man and the woman that there were two huge speaking engagement contracts offered to the company and that they were expected to deliver a speech each in a football stadium full of people. If they speak well, the company and the man and woman would receive accolades and more speaking contracts. If they don't speak well, their reputation would fail, and the company will fire them for losing the contracts. The man and woman gladly accepted the challenge. They were to speak at the same time at two different stadiums.

However, the night before the huge speeches, there was a fire in the apartment complex where the man and woman both lived. The two watches were destroyed.

The next day, the speaking engagements were held. The man did not speak well, because he did not have his magical watch that allows him to speak well. He had relied on his watch to give speeches, and he had never properly learned to speak publicly. The client was disappointed, the man's reputation failed, and his company fired him because he can no longer speak publicly.

On the other hand, the woman also lost her watch in the fire, but she was still able to deliver a perfect speech because she had perfected the art of public speaking through her 100 speaking engagements required by the watch. She was promoted to be vice-president of her company.

A school of fish

A group of fish swimming together is called a school of fish. Fish swimming together has many benefits; one of them is protection from predators. One day, Silly the fish, a member of the school of fish, decided he wanted to leave and go on an adventure on his own.

"But Silly, it will be dangerous for you to go off by yourself," said Silly's fish friends. But Silly didn't listen to them. He left and ventured off by himself.

Later the school of fish, because of their many eyes, spotted a predator lurking in the mud. They escaped.

But poor Silly, when a predator lurks in the mud and he wasn't paying attention, wasn't so lucky.

The well

A woman fell into a well. Fortunately for her, the well was dry and she was not hurt. She shouted as loud as he could, and someone came to her rescue.

"Don't worry, I'll save you!" shouted the man at the top of the well. Then he proceeded to dump buckets of water into the well.

"What are you doing? Are you trying to drown me?" The woman complained as she got drenched in water.

"Don't worry, you will be safe soon," replied the man.

Slowly but surely, the water level rose in the well. The woman floated on the water until the water level was high enough for her to climb out.

The animal trap and a benevolent man

A bear fell into a hunter's trap that had metal teeth snapped shut like a pair of jaws that dug into the bear's leg. The bear roared in pain, and pushed with all its might hoping to get free, but it could not free itself from the trap.

A kind-hearted man saw the poor bear and decided to set it free. To set the bear free, he had to push the trap deeper into the bear's leg before the trap sprung open. The bear did not know and thought the man was trying to hurt it. Once the trap sprung open, the bear then ran off into the hills.

Bookkeeping & Accounting Explained

FREE book sample from:

"Bookkeeping and Accounting Step-by-step Basics for Small & Medium sized Businesses and Home Businesses: Over 20 Examples of Common Accounting Transactions!"

©2015 Calvin Lee
All rights reserved

This book or any portion thereof may not be reproduced or used without written permission of the author/publisher except in brief quotations, book reviews, and articles.

BOOKKEEPING AND ACCOUNTING STEP-BY-STEP BASICS FOR SMALL & MEDIUM SIZED BUSINESSES AND HOME BUSINESSES

CALVIN K. LEE, MBA, CPA

Over 20 examples of common accounting transactions! (Book #6)

Praise for *"Bookkeeping and Accounting Step-by-step Basics for Small & Medium Sized Businesses and Home Businesses"*

"This is awesome! I love the short chapters with clear examples."

"I'm 100% certain to say that this book should be accounting 100 pre-requisite course for anyone who wants to take introduction to accounting! Very clear, concise, and concrete. Well done!"

 - K.T., CPA, CA

Praise from readers of Calvin's books:

"Very practical, good reading!"

"I really enjoy your books."

"Well done, very informative. I like how you used your example."

"By using his own example, Calvin gives hope for the readers."

"Great real life experience that you can relate to easily."

"Very clear, concise, and concrete. Well done."

"Practical tips and relatable examples. A pleasant read. Congratulations on your recent publications! Keep writing more."

"I've taken notes on my smart phone and will implement them in my life."

"Thanks for the little pearls of wisdom and optimism."

Bookkeeping & Accounting Explained

Table of Contents

Introduction

Your first day on the job as a bookkeeper or accountant

Types of accounts in accounting

Balance sheet and income statement

Debits and credits must equal

Assets

Liabilities

Revenue

Expenses

Taxes

Accounts receivable

Accounts payable

Purchasing inventory

Inventory costing methods

Lower of cost or market (LCM)

Capital assets

Depreciation of capital assets

Sale of an asset

Shareholder loans – shareholder pays out of pocket

Shareholder loans – company pays on behalf of shareholder

Year-end closing

About the author

Note to the reader

Contact the author

Introduction

After reading this book, you will be able to do basic bookkeeping with confidence.

Accounting is the language of business. Whether the company is a global Fortune 500 company or a local mom and pop shop, both of these companies need a system to keep track of income, expenses, assets purchased like computers or furniture, liabilities obtained like mortgages, and equity components such as number of shares issued or how much the owner has invested in the company. Of course, the bigger the company and the more transactions it has, the more complex the accounting.

Small & medium sized businesses and home businesses do not need sophisticated accounting software. They just need a simple system to keep track of the company's transactions. This book is written for beginners to accounting and bookkeeping.

I am a designated CPA accountant in both Canada and the U.S., and have worked since 2007 as an accountant and auditor in public accounting firms and companies. The majority of my clients were small to medium sized businesses. Some of my clients' bookkeepers struggle with the accounting software and the basic accounting concepts.

I have also taught accounting courses at York University's reputable Schulich School of Business in Toronto while I was obtaining a MBA degree myself there. I taught in the Bachelor of Business Administration (BBA) program and Master of Accounting (MAcc) program.

I enjoyed teaching accounting concepts to first year students, and I understand that many of them struggle to learn the accounting language. Textbooks are sometimes long and difficult to follow. My greatest satisfaction in teaching is to explain a concept that is challenging a student, and watch a proverbial light bulb light up as they begin to understand the concept.

Since you've picked up this book, I believe you want to learn the basic concepts of accounting and bookkeeping for small & medium sized enterprises and home businesses. *I will use the simplest language to explain basic concepts so that you can perform accounting and bookkeeping duties for your business or company.*

This book is designed to be as practical as possible, so I'm going to focus on application rather than explaining detailed theory and concepts.

Think of this book as a quick reference guide rather than a detailed textbook. Therefore, it does not cover all the topics in a first year accounting course. This book covers the most common transactions an entry accountant or bookkeeper will do on a daily basis.

Bookkeeping & Accounting Explained

FREE book sample from:

"Understanding Financial Statement Analysis for Accountants, Business Owners, Investors, and Stakeholders"

Calvin K. Lee, MBA, CPA, CA, CPA (Illinois)

©2015 Calvin Lee
All rights reserved

This book or any portion thereof may not be reproduced or used without written permission of the author/publisher except in brief quotations, book reviews, and articles.

Look inside ↓

Understanding Financial Statement Analysis

For Accountants, Business Owners, Investors, and Stakeholders

Calvin K. Lee, MBA, CPA, CA

Bookkeeping & Accounting Explained

Table of Contents
1. What you'll get out of this book
2. Balance Sheet - things to watch for
3. Parts of the balance sheet
4. Is lots of cash always a good thing? Not always.
5. Accounts receivable and sales are going up. Great? Maybe not.
6. Inventory - beware of obsolescence
7. Current assets - your first line of defense in business liquidity
8. Current ratio: can this company survive 1 year?
9. Long-term assets - needed to generate future income
10. Property, plant and equipment (PP&E) - watch how they depreciate
11. Intangible assets - essential for some businesses
12. Goodwill - test for impairment
13. Total assets - read the notes and make sure they are all there
14. Return on Assets - did the company make money?
15. Asset turnover ratio - how much revenue did the company make?
16. Current liabilities - pay or face consequences
17. Accounts payable - keep your cash. Delaying payment is good
18. Income taxes payable - do this legally to avoid going to jail
19. Customers' deposits / deferred revenue - not your money...yet!
20. Debts - are they bad or good? It depends
21. Short-term loans - necessary at crucial times
22. Long-term liabilities - a way to fund the business
23. Debt-to-equity ratio - screw this up at your own risk
24. Shareholder's equity - who owns the company?
25. Return on equity - getting your investment money's worth
26. Income statement
27. Revenue - first thing most people look at

28. Cost of sales - let's keep this low
29. Gross margin / gross profit - did we make a profit?
30. Cash flows - cash is king
Final thoughts
Bonus video on balance sheet concepts
Note to the reader

1. What you'll get out of this book

After reading this book you should have a good understanding of financial statements and reports.

Accounting is the basic language of business. Whether you are an accountant/bookkeeper, a business owner, or an investor, you look at financial statements and reports to determine how well a company is performing.

As a CPA, I look at financial statements every day. I also prepare financial statements for clients. I will share with you in simple terms how to understand and make use of financial statements to achieve your goals.

Where do you start?

Financial statements have several components, including the balance sheet, income statement, cash flow statement, statement of equity, and notes to financial statements.

In my job as a public accountant/auditor I've worked with many different companies. On many days I work with new clients. I have to familiarize myself with the company before doing my audit work.

I start by looking at the notes to the financial statements, usually attached at the end of the financial statements. The notes generally give a good overview of what the company does and introduces the many features in the balance sheet and income statement.

If you're an accountant or bookkeeper who's looking to not only understand financial statements, but also understand the bookkeeping/accounting principles, I suggest you read this book and also my book _"Bookkeeping and Accounting Step-by-step Basics for Small & Medium Sized Businesses and Home Businesses: Over 20 Examples of Common Accounting Transactions!"_ (click here to get a copy in Amazon). In that book I show you the basics of how to do bookkeeping.

Bonus video on balance sheet to further explain concepts at the end of this book! Click here to go to end of book now. There will be a link back here.

2. Balance Sheet - things to watch for

The balance sheet is a historical statement. It is a snapshot at a particular time, usually the year-end of the company.

The balance sheet is usually prepared in the time right after the year-end, usually due for filing with the government 2 or 3 months after the year-end.

Example.
Let's say a company has a year-end of December 31. If you are an investor you are entitled to a copy of the financial statements. Let's say you're an investor looking to invest in a company. You get the financial statements in March of the next year.

You have to remember that the financial statements show the financial performance of a company as at December 31. What has happened in the few months after is not reflected on the financial statements.

If there was a lawsuit that happened subsequent to the date of the financial statements, it would not show on the balance sheet. If the company was sold subsequent to the financial statements date, it would not show on the balance sheet. If new technology was introduced subsequent to the financial statements date, it would not show on the balance sheet.

How to account for these subsequent events?

There are several ways. On the notes to the financial statements, there is a section where management may disclose some foreseeable subsequent events. Another way is to try to get interim financial statements for the new fiscal year subsequent to the year-end financial statements.

URL letter: w

3. Parts of the balance sheet

The balance sheet is generally divided into three main parts. They are:
- Assets
- Liabilities
- Equity

Assets represent the tangible and intangible assets of a company. Tangible assets are things like cash and inventory. Intangible assets include things like goodwill, which is formed when a company purchases another company at a price higher than the net assets of the company being acquired.

Why would a company pay a price higher than the net assets?

It's because the company being acquired has a brand or existing customer list that is worth something and valuable to the company that is acquiring, but these items are not listed on the balance sheet of the company being acquired.

URL letter: a

4. Is lots of cash always a good thing? Not always.

The first asset that is listed is usually cash. Many users of the financial statements, such as accountants/bookkeepers, business owners, investors, creditors, and other stakeholders, look at the amount of cash on hand.

A large cash balance is always good, right?

Wrong. Having a lot of cash on the balance sheet may indicate poor management. Let me explain.

Example.
Cash is sometimes listed as "cash and cash equivalents", meaning any short term liquid investments like certificate of deposits of 30 days are included as "cash". Idle cash doesn't help the company grow its asset base. Perhaps it is better if management puts excess idle cash into investments. I've seen this with some companies. They have lots of cash just sitting there when they should invest it in investments or do something else to make use of their excess cash.

Conclusion:
Unless there is a good reason for the cash balance to be large, such as expecting to pay a large bill or make a purchase, a large cash balance could indicate poor management.

URL letter: t

5. Accounts receivable and sales are going up. Great? Maybe not.

A business usually receives payment from customers in several different forms, including cash or on credit, or a combination of the two.

Accounts receivable is a customer promising to pay in the future in exchange for goods or services now. When a business or company starts up, initially it may grant lenient credit policies to attract more customers.

When customers with lower credit rating are allowed to purchase goods or services on credit, there will usually be more sales. The sales on the income statement increases, and so does accounts receivable. Everything is fine, and business is booming, right?

Maybe.

Example.
A large accounts receivable is useless to a company if they cannot collect cash from customers who promise to pay later. Remember cash is king. If a company doesn't receive cash from its customers, it doesn't matter how many millions of dollars of sales it is generating.

A company must still pay its bills and creditors regardless whether it is collecting cash from its customers or not. Some companies in an attempt to grow sales have done exactly what was described above. But when the company's cash reserves run out, creditors will call loans, and the company may need to fold even though it is generating a lot of sales.

Conclusion:
To put it simply, a large accounts receivable can be a good thing, or it can be a warning sign.

As long as a company can keep collecting cash from its customers listed on the accounts receivable, then it is not in immediate danger. If customers are taking more than 90 days to pay, then the company may have some collection issues.

URL letter: c

BONUS BOOK #6:

"LEAP before you THINK"

Bookkeeping & Accounting Explained

Look inside ↓

Calvin K. Lee, MBA, CPA

LEAP before you THINK

Most of us live pretty ordinary lives. Every day we go to work, get off from work, and look forward to the weekend. Every day is so predictable it becomes dreadful, monotonous, boring. We do things on autopilot, and our minds are off wandering elsewhere.

Opportunities come, and opportunities go. Let's pretend the perfect opportunity suddenly showed up in front of you right now, and you have 30 seconds to make up your mind. What would you do?

Most people would panic, because it was not part of the plan. People hesitate, become scared, become reluctant, start asking "what if", and repeat the cycle in their head until they've talked themselves out of it.

Why don't 97% of us live exciting, extraordinary lives? What's holding us back?

FEAR.

Fear holds most of us back. What do we fear? Fear of the unknown. Fear of failure. Fear of rejection. Fear of success. Fear of what others think of us. Fear that we won't know what to do, what to say. Fear that we embarrass ourselves. Fear of ridicule.

What's your fear?

Fear is like a bubble surrounding us. It serves to protects us, but it also prevents 97% of us from realizing our dreams, our potential, our goals, and our destiny.

The good news is, if you can conquer the fear in your life, you gain unlimited power and potential to gain wealth, health, happiness, success, and freedom.

How did fear come into our lives? Most new born children are fearless. They're not afraid of heights as they climbed up the kitchen cabinet to reach for that cookie jar. They're not afraid of saying stupid things. They're not worried about what others think of them when they cry. Children are fearless. They will try anything anywhere, anytime.

But somewhere along the way as we grew up we inherited our fears from other people. We are told that highways are dangerous. We are told that people around us are out to take advantage of us. We are told that we shouldn't dream stupid dreams and become stable and get a steady job. We are taught in school that making a mistake means we are a failure and should feel bad.

Most of us live in a prison in our mind. We are a prisoner of what others think of us. We are so worried about what others think that we dress, act, think, and speak in a way that is socially acceptable. We conform. We lose our uniqueness. We lose ourselves.

The result? We try to blend in. We want to be part of the crowd. We don't want to take risks. We stay in our comfort zone.

Yet deep inside, each of us have a fire inside of us. We have our passions that have been tucked away for so long. That passion may be to learn a new instrument, live in a foreign country, attend graduate school, run for president of the charity we volunteer at, or quit your job and start a business.

We wish...we wish...

And it never happens if we stay wishing. Never. Nada.

LEAP BEFORE YOU THINK

In order to actually feel alive, we must do something. Do anything. It's okay to take baby steps as long as you're moving.

Once you have an idea of what you want to do, you must start to do it. Too many people stop after they dream. They start thinking about the 1,000,000 reasons why they will fail. The longer they think, the more reasons they come up with.

Sometimes the remedy for this paralysis by analysis is to LEAP before you THINK. If you really want to become president of that charity you volunteer at, LEAP before you THINK. Even if you're not sure if you

have all the qualifications, raise your hand and volunteer. Believe you can do it.

If you want to live in a foreign country, LEAP before you THINK. Start filling out visa applications, start booking airplane tickets, and fulfill your dream. If you think too much, you won't go anywhere. You know what I'm saying is true because you've procrastinated before.

I have used the LEAP before you THINK strategy numerous times and it has worked wonders. The above two examples are actually real events from my own life where I used the LEAP before you THINK strategy.

In September 2011, I started volunteering at the Institute of Chartered Accountants of British Columbia. I was a freshly designated professional accountant. I was young, inexperienced, but full of hope and excitement for the future. I started volunteering for the Young Chartered Accountants (CA) Forum because 1) I was a young CA myself, and 2) The committee needed new members, fresh blood who had new and innovative ideas.

In the summer of 2012, the previous Chair of the Young CA Forum decided to step down. The staff liaison at the Institute of Chartered Accountants of British Columbia asked if there were any volunteers to step up and take over as Chair. There were about 15 CA's on the committee. Any one of us can become the new Chair.

I remember hesitating for a moment. I really wanted to spread my wings and test my leadership skills. In the past, I've volunteered as president of clubs, but I've never volunteered at the professional level. The doubts started mounting:

Who am I?

Am I experienced enough?

Do I have what it takes?

What if I fail?

Then I remembered why I joined the Young CA Forum. I wanted to organize educational events to help other young professionals achieve their career goals. I believed I can lead the Young CA Forum as their Chair.

I LEAP before I THINK. I raised my hand and volunteered.

It's interesting how our fear subsides once the decision is made and set. Our minds are amazing tools - our minds can find new innovative ways to solve problems once we set our minds to them. We give ourselves too little credit, and we are often our own worst critiques. By doing LEAP before you THINK, you don't permit your mind enough time to come up with the 1,000,000 reasons why you shouldn't LEAP. In fact, courage comes right after you LEAP before you THINK.

The second example is when I moved to a foreign country and lived there for a year. I was studying my MBA degree in Toronto in 2013 when the opportunity to go study abroad came up. Peking University, China's top university, offered me admission with full scholarship into their newly developed Double MBA degree program to start in 2014. I pioneered this new Double MBA degree program between York University in Toronto, Canada, and Peking University in Beijing, China. No one has done it before me, but because I pioneered this program, I hope others can follow in my footsteps.

I would usually be afraid of leaving the comfort of my own country and go live in a foreign country with a foreign language, foreign culture, far far away from friends and family. I decided to LEAP before I THINK. I just believed God would help me overcome all obstacles and that I would succeed. To be honest, I didn't know how difficult it was going to be. As a pioneer of the new program, the very first Double MBA degree student going from York to Peking, a lot of things had to be ironed out. Double MBA degree students that come after me would not know all the problems I faced as I forged a new path for myself and for them.

****

Was it hard? Yes.

Was it worth it? Definitely. Absolutely. 100% yes.

****

To this day, I can talk about my experiences and inspire others to do things they didn't think possible. *I encourage others to LEAP before they THINK. Of course, LEAP before you THINK involves carefully calculating and assessing risk. LEAP before you THINK means to be brave, be courageous, be bold. Don't THINK too long because the longer you think, the less likely you'll be able to LEAP.*

****

Repeat this mantra to yourself:

LEAP before you THINK

LEAP before you THINK

LEAP before you THINK

****

Commit this LEAP before you THINK mantra to memory, and use it often. You'll be amazed at the results. You'll feel so much more alive. You'll finally be able to do the things you've always wanted to do but were too afraid to do. You will fail sometimes, but that's okay. Just get back up and try again. No one who has ever become great did so without failing a lot. They failed much worse than you.

I've failed numerous times in my life. I've been rejected many times, I've fallen and learned my lessons, and I've picked myself back up. I've felt that I was a total failure. I've felt that I could no longer get back up. I've felt I've lost all hope. I've been there, done that.

Many people see other people's successes and think they did so without any failure. The truth is, the more successful someone is, the more failures they've experienced along the way. Read the biographies of famous people who have succeeded in politics, business, sports, etc. and you'll see that they struggled

a lot in many aspects. What's to be admired is their perseverance to continue to LEAP.

If you ask any of these famous people whether their efforts were worth it, I'm sure they will say yes. If you ask them did they figure everything out before they started, they'd probably say no. Most people learn along the way. They believe they can do it even though no one has done it before. They pay their tuition of their learning through failing, and getting back up. But the key is that they chose to LEAP before they THINK. If they just sit there and not LEAP, they would never succeed.

Final words

Today, what will you do?

The choice is yours.

Live life without regret. Do it now. Don't wait another moment.

LEAP before you THINK

LEAP before you THINK

LEAP before you THINK

Bookkeeping & Accounting Explained

FREE Book sample from

"TIME MANAGEMENT: saving 4 HOURS a week"

Look inside ↓

Table of Contents

Praise from readers

Table of Contents

1) Do you want to save 4 hours a week?

2) Trip bundling

3) Leaving work earlier or later than rush hour

4) Get started on assignments sooner

5) Organize your closet

6) Organize when washing dishes

7) E-mail scheduling

8) Make a list

9) Organize your desk

10) Delegate

11) Learn to say no

12) Turn off that smart phone

13) Learn to use computer shortcuts

14) Stop worrying

15) Plan your week on Sunday or Monday morning

16) Keep learning life hacks

17) Get your clothes ready the night before

18) Limit the time

19) Do something when you're waiting

20) Prepare in batches

21) Plan your travels

22) Avoid travelling during peak seasons

23) Don't worry about perfection

24) Aim to understand, not memorize

25) Shopping during non-peak hours

26) Create an index or table of contents

27) Do regular maintenance

28) Wash the plates immediately, or at least rinse them

29) Create your own system

30) Upgrade your equipment

31) Be more knowledgeable

Final thoughts

1. Do you want to save 4 HOURS a week?

Does it feel like you **don't have enough time** to do everything on your to-do list?

Do you wish a day has more than **24 hours**?

If so, you should read this book. This book will provide ways that you can save time throughout your week. There is a suggestion for every day of a 30 day month. You can use as many or as few as you like. If you use just 2 suggestions in this book, you can easily save 4 HOURS a week. If you use all 30, you'll become a master of time management and can start doing the things you really want to with all your time savings.

What would you do with an additional 4 HOURS a week?

That's enough to watch a *Lord of the Rings* movie or *King Kong* by Peter Jackson. You can take a nap. You can read a book or magazine. You can meet up with friends. You can spend some quality time with your spouse or children.

I use all of these tips below myself. My friends say I am one of the most efficient people they know. On top of a full-time job as a CPA professional accountant, I was chair of the Young Professionals Forum committee at the CPA institute, served as a leader and organizer for the CPA Social Networking Group, served as a board member for a charity, and volunteered at church.

In this book I share with you how I can do it all. The key is in time management.

2. Trip bundling

The first way to save time is to bundle your trips to a similar area. For example, you have to go to the grocery store on Saturday, and you also want to meet up with a couple friends on separate occasions. One lives near the grocery store, and the other lives in another part of town. If you had the choice, schedule to meet the friend that lives near the grocery store right before or after your grocery stop trip. That way, you save the time of making two separate trips: getting prepared to leave the house, and the time to drive there and back.

If getting prepared to leave the house takes you 20 minutes and driving takes you 20 minutes, to and fro means 40 minutes. Altogether, you save an hour if you bundle your two trips (grocery store and meeting friend that lives near grocery store).

I use this trip bundling strategy often. If I have to go downtown to meet someone, I try to book another meeting with someone else on the same trip. It takes me about 30 minutes one way to get downtown, on top of getting prepared to leave the house. By bundling multiple meetings, I save over an hour than if I make two trips at two different times to meet two different people.

Using this method, you can save at least 1 hour a week.

----

3. Leaving work earlier or later than rush hour

Rush hour in my city starts in the morning around 8:30am. If I go to work an hour and a half earlier (7am) or an hour and a half later (10am), there is practically no traffic. My 30 minute drive usually becomes 45 minutes or more during traffic jam times.

Rush hour in the evening starts at about 5pm. If I leave two hours before (3pm) or two hours after (7pm), there is practically no traffic. During rush hour, my 30 minute drive becomes 45 minutes or more.

If I save 15 minutes in the morning and 15 minutes in the evening just by avoiding rush hour, I save 30 minutes a day, 5 times a week means 150 minutes, or 2.5 hours a week. Multiply that by 50 weeks a year means over 100 hours saved per year just by making this small adjustment.

Using this method, you can save 2.5 hours a week.

Bookkeeping & Accounting Explained

FREE book sample from:
From Ordinary to Extraordinary:
How God Used Ordinary Men and Women in the Bible

From Ordinary to Extraordinary:

How God Used Ordinary Men and Women in the Bible

With 3 bonus books!

Calvin K. Lee, MBA, CPA

©2015 Calvin Lee
All Rights Reserved

To my friends: may love, joy, peace and hope follow you all the days of your lives.

This book or any portion thereof may not be reproduced or used without written permission of the author/publisher except in brief quotations, book reviews, and articles.

Scripture quotations are taken from the Holy Bible, New International Version®, NIV®.
Copyright © 1973, 1978, 1984, 2011 by Biblica, Inc.™

Bookkeeping & Accounting Explained

Table of Contents

1. God uses ordinary men and women in the Bible. Joseph, Moses, Hannah, Elijah, Gideon, Esther, Rahab, David, Jeremiah, Jonah, Peter, Matthew, Paul

2. All extraordinary people used by God have flaws. Moses, David, Solomon, Samson, Peter, Paul

3. Too old? Moses was 80 years old. Abraham, Caleb, Joshua

4. Too young? The virgin Mary was 12 years old. Jeremiah, David, Samuel

5. No money? The widow's olive oil

6. Expect miracles: the men and women didn't have to figure out how God does things. Mary, Gideon, Daniel's friends

7. God shapes character for service. Joseph, David, Moses

8. Our timing is not God's timing. Isaiah 55

9. Lack education or training or qualifications? Moses, Joseph, Peter, John

10. Even if one is extraordinary, he or she still needs a supportive team. Moses, Aaron, Hur

11. Getting prepared to be an extraordinary Christian. Joshua, Psalms

12. Sin may be preventing one from being an extraordinary man or woman of God. King Nebuchadnezzar

13. Bible verses on becoming an extraordinary Christian. 1 Peter, Jeremiah, Psalms

14. I'm living an extraordinary life - why do I still face troubles? Job, Elijah

15. Living an extraordinary life in times of pain. Job

16. Maintaining an extraordinary life. John, Isaiah

17. Don't compare - everyone's extraordinary life is different.

18. Leaving a legacy - preparing the next generation for an extraordinary life. From Moses to Joshua, Elijah to Elisha, Jesus to his 12 disciples

Final thoughts

1. God uses ordinary men and women in the Bible. Joseph, Moses, Hannah, Elijah, Gideon, Esther, Rahab, David, Jeremiah, Jonah, Peter, Matthew, Paul

In the Bible are recorded numerous stories of how God took ordinary men and women and made them extraordinary. Think about some prominent men and women in the Bible. Which characters comes to mind?

Examples.
- Joseph was a slave and imprisoned two years, yet God made him prime minister over Egypt.

- Moses complained he was slow in words, yet God made him a great leader over Israel. Moses also in his anger destroyed the stone plates where God Himself had written the Ten Commandments.

- Hannah was deeply troubled and wept as her rival provoked her to irritate her, yet she gave birth to the great prophet Samuel.

- Elijah was depressed, yet God made him one of only two people who never experienced physical death.

- Gideon doubted and tested God, yet the angel of God called him "mighty warrior."

- Esther was from the smallest tribe of Israel, yet God made her queen and she saved her people from evil.

- Rahab was a prostitute, yet she is an ancestor of Jesus (Matthew 1:5)

- David was an adulterer, yet God called him "a man after my own heart."

- Jeremiah said to God, "I do not know how to speak; I am only a child," (Jeremiah 1:6) yet God made him a great prophet.

- Jonah fled from God, yet God entrusted him with an important mission to convert a whole city.

- Peter was a coward, yet Jesus called him a "rock".

- Matthew was a "sinner" despised by all men, yet Jesus called him to follow him.

- Paul murdered Christians before his conversion, yet he wrote at least 13 of the 27 books in the New Testament.

- Jesus himself was a carpenter, born in a lowly manger, yet God exalted him at the highest place and Jesus sits at the right hand of God.

The list can go on and on how God took ordinary men and women and He used them extraordinarily in His plans. God doesn't always call the equipped, the talented, the gifted. But He always equips those he calls to do his work.

Remember:
God doesn't call the equipped. God equips the called.

You may think you are just one ordinary person who doesn't have what it takes to make a difference in this world. If you look at it from a limited human being's point of view, that may be what you see. But God's point of view may be completely different. He doesn't look at what skills and abilities you have. He looks at the heart, and if the person has the right heart to do God's work, God will provide everything he or she needs.

Rarely does anyone being called by God is completely ready. Faith is living life walking with God step by step as He works in us to remove our impurities and rough edges. From the Bible we can see that God enjoys using ordinary people - people with no special talents. If God calls someone with innate talent, that person may think he or she completed the works by his or her own abilities, not God's. That's why God calls the weak, so that they can rely on His strength, and they can witness how powerful God is. He takes ordinary people to do extraordinary things.

There is a saying, *no pain, no gain.* Often going from ordinary to extraordinary involves some growing pains. In order to grow, we must stretch ourselves beyond our current state mentally, physically, emotionally, and spiritually. We can't stay in our current ordinary state and expect to become extraordinary. God didn't promise life to be easy, but He did promise He will be with us.

If we allow God to work in our lives, He will make our lives extraordinary. It first starts with listening to God and observe what He is doing. So often we are caught up in our busy lives that we neglect listening to God's quiet voice. God is a gentleman, He doesn't shout loudly at us to get our attention. In order to hear God's voice and start our journey to becoming extraordinary, we need to first quiet ourselves and build a relationship with God.

Sometimes we start off on our journey from ordinary to extraordinary, and then we stop short of getting to extraordinary.

Example.
Abraham's father was on his way from ordinary to extraordinary as he set off to travel to Canaan, God's promised land. However, he stopped short of getting there.

Genesis 11:31-32

[31] Terah took his son Abram, his grandson Lot son of Haran, and his daughter-in-law Sarai, the wife of his son Abram, and together they set out from Ur of the Chaldeans to go to Canaan. But when they came to Harran, they settled there.

[32] Terah lived 205 years, and he died in Harran.

Terah set out for Canaan, but he settled half way in Harran and died there. Canaan was God's promised land for His people. Five books later in the Bible in Joshua 14:1 it says:

Now these are the areas the Israelites received as an inheritance in the land of Canaan, which Eleazar the priest, Joshua son of Nun and the heads of the tribal clans of Israel allotted to them. (Joshua 14:1)

Perhaps Abraham's father felt it was comfortable to live in Harran, and perhaps he thought that it wasn't worth the effort and discomfort of getting to Canaan, the land of flowing milk and honey.

***

The problem of stopping half way between ordinary to extraordinary is that we don't receive all the blessings that God intends us to receive. Again, God is a gentleman. He doesn't force us to receive His blessings. He can tell us what He has in store for us, but it is up to us to decide whether to receive it or not.

It's similar to whether we choose to receive Christ or not into our lives. God lets us choose whether we want to continue living our mundane ordinary lives, or live an extraordinary life with Him.

Living an extraordinary life often involves a certain amount of risk, and stepping out of our comfort zone. The Apostle Peter could have chosen to turn down Jesus' invitation to follow Him. If Peter did that, he would have lived the rest of his life as an ordinary fisherman. Instead, Peter took the courage and a leap of faith to follow Christ, and lived an extraordinary life. He lived with Christ and was monumental in building the early church. His life transformed the lives of so many others, and he left a legacy for those who followed after him.

When going from ordinary to extraordinary, our attitude is very important. We can't just *hope or wish* to live an extraordinary life. We have to *expect* to live an extraordinary life. God won't just passively drop an extraordinary life on your lap. Living an extraordinary life involves action on our part. It involves change. It involves some discomfort. But the outcome and result is well worth the effort over one-hundred times.

One of the greatest regrets dying people have is not following their heart, and just living an ordinary life. Nurses in caring homes have reported that they hear the same regrets from dying people over and over again. The dying wish they had taken more risks in life. They wish they had more courage to do the things they really wanted to do. Another words, they regretted staying put in being ordinary. They wished they had made better decisions during their lives to live more extraordinarily. But it is too late.

As you're reading this book, I hope it's not too late for you. You still have time to change and go from ordinary to extraordinary. Whether you're 12 years old or 80 years old, *now* is the time to do something. In this book, I give examples of people who are as young as 12 years old and as old as 80 years old when their ordinary life changed to become extraordinary. The 12 year old is the virgin Mary, mother of Jesus. The 80 year old is Moses, who led the Israelites out of Egypt.

There is no best time to live an extraordinary life. If you keep waiting it may never come. Decide *now* that you will live an extraordinary life and ask God to work in and through you. You may be pleasantly surprised at what blessings God pours out in your life once you start asking and expecting great things.

You may be thinking *I'll start living an extraordinary life when*:

- I graduate from college
- I get that promotion
- I get married
- My last child leaves the house

Maybe the things above make your life extraordinary - if that is you, congratulations. But it is so easy to postpone living an extraordinary life. When we think the time has come, more things happen and we keep postponing our dreams of living an extraordinary life. If you've lived through several stages of life, you know what I'm talking about that life only gets busier.

Let's look at how God used ordinary men and women in the Bible, and turned their lives from ordinary to extraordinary.

2. All extraordinary people used by God have flaws. Moses, David, Solomon, Samson, Peter, Paul

Some of you may have grown up in church and heard all the Bible stories about the heroes of the Bible and how God used them in His great works.

Name a few important characters.

You may name Moses, King David, King Solomon, Samson, Peter, Paul, and the list goes on and on.

Were these people perfect? No.

Did they have any character flaws? Yes.

Let's take a look at some examples.

Example.
Moses is one of the greatest leaders in the history of Israel. He led the Israelites out of Egypt, and performed great miracles like parting the red sea. But Moses had flaws, include a fatal flaw that made God angry that God wouldn't let him into the promised land.

Deuteronomy 34:4-5
4 Then the LORD said to him, "This is the land I promised on oath to Abraham, Isaac and Jacob when I said, 'I will give it to your descendants.' I have let you see it with your eyes, but you will not cross over into it."

5 And Moses the servant of the LORD died there in Moab, as the LORD had said.

What were some of Moses' flaws?

First, when God called him Moses during the burning bush incident Moses tried to shed responsibility and asked God to send someone else by saying he doesn't know how to speak.

Exodus 4:10-14

[10] Moses said to the LORD, "Pardon your servant, Lord. I have never been eloquent, neither in the past nor since you have spoken to your servant. I am slow of speech and tongue."

[11] The LORD said to him, "Who gave human beings their mouths? Who makes them deaf or mute? Who gives them sight or makes them blind? Is it not I, the LORD? [12] Now go; I will help you speak and will teach you what to say."

[13] But Moses said, "Pardon your servant, Lord. Please send someone else."

[14] Then the LORD's anger burned against Moses and he said, "What about your brother, Aaron the Levite? I know he can speak well. He is already on his way to meet you, and he will be glad to see you.

Notice in verse 14 the Lord's anger burned against Moses. Moses had his flaws and sometimes made God angry.

Second, when Moses was up in the mountain receiving the Ten Commandments from God, his brother Aaron made a golden calf for the Israelites to worship. This made Moses so mad that when he came down from the mountain with the stone tablets of the Ten Commandments which God wrote with His own finger, Moses threw the stone tablets out of his hands and breaking them.

Exodus 32:19

¹⁹ When Moses approached the camp and saw the calf and the dancing, his anger burned and he threw the tablets out of his hands, breaking them to pieces at the foot of the mountain.

Third, and this is the fatal error Moses made, Moses did not trust God enough to honor Him as holy in the sight of the Israelites. God said this Himself in Numbers 20:11.

Numbers 20:8-12

> ₈"Take the staff, and you and your brother Aaron gather the assembly together. Speak to that rock before their eyes and it will pour out its water. You will bring water out of the rock for the community so they and their livestock can drink."
>
> ₉So Moses took the staff from the LORD's presence, just as he commanded him. ₁₀He and Aaron gathered the assembly together in front of the rock and Moses said to them, "Listen, you rebels, must we bring you water out of this rock?" ₁₁Then Moses raised his arm and struck the rock twice with his staff. Water gushed out, and the community and their livestock drank.
>
> ₁₂But the LORD said to Moses and Aaron, "Because you did not trust in me enough to honor me as holy in the sight of the Israelites, you will not bring this community into the land I give them."

Here, God clearly gave instructions in verse 8 for Moses to speak to the rock in front of the Israelites and the rock will pour out water. However, Moses struck the rock twice with his staff. God was disappointed with Moses for not trusting in God enough that Moses will not set foot in the promised land.

Example.

Bookkeeping & Accounting Explained

King David is one of the best known characters in the Bible. He was God's anointed king over Israel, and David reigned forty years (1 Kings 2:11).

David did many great things for God. But he also had many faults.

Perhaps his biggest mistake was committing adultery with Bathsheba. Bathsheba was a married woman, and one day David spotted her from his palace bathing on a roof. David sent messengers to get her, and he slept with her. Then he murdered her husband. See 2 Samuel 11 for the full account of the story.

Another fault of David can be seen in 1 Chronicles 21. David takes a census and counts the number of fighting men in his army. This was evil in the sight of God, and He punished Israel, giving David the choice between 3 punishments:

1) 3 years of famine
2) 3 months of being swept away before their enemies
3) 3 days of plague

In the end, God sent a plague that killed 70,000 men of Israel. The angel of the Lord nearly destroyed Jerusalem, but God grieved and ordered the angel to withdraw his hand.

Even though David is not perfect, one thing respectable about David is that he doesn't make the same mistake twice. He learns from his mistakes, and doesn't make the same mistake again.

As we can see, even if we're anointed by God, we still will encounter troubles and problems. David was pursued by enemies, and in the Psalms over and over again he laments to God about his enemies plotting against him.

Example.
Solomon was the wisest man who ever lived. He built the temple of the Lord, and had all the splendor and glory. However, he too, had human flaws, as we see in 1 Kings chapter 11.

1 Kings 11:1-13

Solomon's Wives

₁King Solomon, however, loved many foreign women besides Pharaoh's daughter—Moabites, Ammonites, Edomites, Sidonians and Hittites. ₂They were from nations about which the LORD had told the Israelites, "You must not intermarry with them, because they will surely turn your hearts after their gods." Nevertheless, Solomon held fast to them in love. ₃He had seven hundred wives of royal birth and three hundred concubines, and his wives led him astray. ₄As Solomon grew old, his wives turned his heart after other gods, and his heart was not fully devoted to the LORD his God, as the heart of David his father had been. ₅He followed Ashtoreth the goddess of the Sidonians, and Molek the detestable god of the Ammonites. ₆So Solomon did evil in the eyes of the LORD; he did not follow the LORD completely, as David his father had done.

₇On a hill east of Jerusalem, Solomon built a high place for Chemosh the detestable god of Moab, and for Molek the detestable god of the Ammonites. ₈He did the same for all his foreign wives, who burned incense and offered sacrifices to their gods.

₉The LORD became angry with Solomon because his heart had turned away from the LORD, the God of Israel, who had appeared to him twice. ₁₀Although he had forbidden Solomon to follow other gods, Solomon did not keep the LORD's command. ₁₁So the LORD said to Solomon, "Since this is your attitude and you have not kept my covenant and my decrees, which I commanded you, I will most certainly tear the kingdom away from you and give it to one of your subordinates. 12Nevertheless, for the sake of David your father, I will not do it during your lifetime. I will tear it out of the hand of your son. 13Yet I will not tear the whole kingdom from him, but will give him one tribe for the sake of David my servant and for the sake of Jerusalem, which I have chosen."

Due to Solomon's flaw of loving and intermarrying with women from other nations that led Solomon's heart away from God, God punished him by tearing his kingdom away from his descendents.

Example.
Samson was a strong man and judge of the Israelites who can kill a lion with his bare hands. Samson fell in love with a woman called Delilah and she tricked him into telling her the secret of his great strength. Delilah then betrayed Samson and his enemies the Philistines and they cut off his hair and the strength of the Lord left him. See Judges 16 for the story of Samson and Delilah.

However, God gave Samson strength one last time before his death, and he killed many Philistines when he pushed over the pillars of the temple.

Example.
Peter was one of the first disciples Jesus called to follow Him. He was a fisherman, an unschooled, impulsive man who acted on his emotions.

An example of when Peter was impulsive is when Jesus was arrested in Gethsemane. Peter drew his sword and cut off the ear of the servant of the high priest (Matthew 26:51).

Peter was a coward who denied Jesus three times, yet Jesus called him "the rock" that he will build his church.

(And I tell you that you are Peter, and on this rock I will build my church, and the gates of Hades will not overcome it. Matthew 16:18)

The Apostle Paul also rebuked Peter for hypocrisy. Let's look at the Bible.

Paul Opposes Peter (Galatians 2:11-13)

[11] When Peter came to Antioch, I opposed him to his face, because he stood condemned. [12] For before certain men came from James, he used to eat with the Gentiles. But when they arrived, he began to draw back and separate himself from the Gentiles because he was afraid of those who belonged to the circumcision group. [13] The other Jews joined him in his hypocrisy, so that by their hypocrisy even Barnabas was led astray.

Conclusion:
Peter was far from perfect. Yet God used Peter greatly and Peter was monumental in the building of the early church.

Example.
Paul is the apostle who wrote many of the letters in the New Testament. But before Paul became a follower of Christ, he persecuted and murdered Christians. But God was able to take a murderer and make him into a blessing for Christians of his time and Christians after his time.

About the Author

Calvin K. Lee, MBA, CPA, CA, CPA (Illinois) is an accountant, author, composer, and teacher. He has lived in Beijing, Hong Kong, Toronto, and Vancouver, and travelled to many countries including the U.S.; to Europe such as the U.K., France, Italy, Germany, and Switzerland; and to Asia such as China, Malaysia, Singapore, Japan, and Thailand. Some of his favorite topics include love, relationships, effective communication, psychology, leadership, teamwork, and business. His biggest passion is inspiring and helping others achieve their goals. To do this, Calvin has been writing articles for his blog for over 10 years to inspire and encourage others.

Calvin holds an undergraduate degree from the University of British Columbia in Vancouver, a MBA degree with distinction from York University in Toronto, Canada and is expecting a Double MBA degree from Peking University in Beijing, China in 2016. He is a CPA designated accountant in the U.S. and Canada, and also a Chartered Accountant in Canada. In addition to his successful career in accounting, he has also taught Master of Accounting classes at university, taught accounting modules at the CPA professional association, and enjoys being a mentor to younger accountants. He has served as President of the MBA Ambassadors during his MBA studies and as Chair of the Young Professionals Forum at the CPA Association.

Contact the author

Want a FREE PDF version of this book? Subscribe to my e-mail list by sending an e-mail with the title in subject line. I will e-mail you a free PDF version of this book. Be sure to include the title in the subject.

Website:
 www.hellocalvinlee.com

Amazon page:
www.amazon.com/author/hellocalvinlee

Blog:
www.hellocalvinlee.com/blog

Facebook:
https://www.facebook.com/hellocalvinlee

E-mail:
hellocalvinlee@gmail.com

Twitter:
@calvinklee2010
www.Twitter.com/calvinklee2010

If there are any topics you want me to write about in a future book, I'd love to know!

I welcome feedback and comments.

Other books by Calvin K. Lee

Visit my website http://www.hellocalvinlee.com to view my other books. See my Amazon author page: www.amazon.com/author/hellocalvinlee.

1. How to Increase Confidence and Succeed in Meeting People: Business Networking the Easy Way: Meet New People Now!

2. Living an Extraordinary and Amazingly Purposeful Life: 9 Principles to a Better Life

3. Words of Wisdom, Encouragement, and Inspiration: Bring Happiness into Your Life

4. How to Work Smarter, Not Harder: Success in the Workplace

5. A Collection of Short Stories: And the Moral of the Story is...?

6. Bookkeeping and Accounting Step-by-step Basics for Small & Medium Sized Businesses and Home Businesses: Over 20 Examples of Common Accounting Transactions!

7. Understanding Financial Statements: For Accountants, Business Owners, Investors, and Stakeholders

8. LEAP before you THINK

9. TIME MANAGEMENT: saving 4 HOURS a week

10. From Ordinary to Extraordinary: How God Used Ordinary Men and Women in the Bible

THANK YOU!

Thank you for reading my book. I really appreciate your time, and I'm sure you'll get something useful out of this book.

To thank you for getting this book, you can get another FREE eBook on Stress Management on my website:

www.hellocalvinlee.com/ebook

Made in the USA
Lexington, KY
28 January 2017